Achieving a PhD
— ten students' experience

Achieving a PhD
— ten students' experience

Phillida Salmon

Trentham Books

First published in 1992 by Trentham Books Limited

Trentham Books Limited
Westview House
734 London Road,
Oakhill, Stoke-on-Trent,
Staffordshire ST4 5NP

Cover design: Trentham Print Design Limited

British Library Cataloguing in Publication Data
Salmon, Phillida
    Achieving a PhD: ten students' experience.
    I. Title
    378.24

ISBN: 0948080 59 0

Designed and typeset by Trentham Print Design Limited, Chester
and printed in Great Britain by BPCC Wheatons Ltd, Exeter.

Contents

Acknowledgements

The following students have contributed to this book:
Qadir Bakhsh, Ian Beadle, Ann Constanti, Maggie Futcher, Grace Leung,
Sheila Macrae, Jocelyn Maximé, Lesley Smith, Chris Thorman, Susan Weil

Front row: (L to R): Ian, Chris, Susan, Jocelyn, Maggie
Back row (L to R): Ann, Lesley, Phil, Sheila, Grace, Qadir

Introduction

This book is written for those who are contemplating doctoral work, or have already embarked on doctoral projects. Becoming a PhD student means entering a peculiarly complex and private situation: it is a world about which few people have spoken. The contributors to the present volume are themselves members of this world, as existing or very recent PhD students. They offer here their reflections on their own first-hand experience, as people aware of the value, as well as the difficulties, of this unique form of learning.

In the context of higher education, PhD students stand out as exceptional in many ways. They are by definition different from the much larger body of students following taught courses, for Diplomas, Bachelors or Masters degrees. Their studies, unlike others, are not prescribed; the content of their work is self-chosen and to a large extent self-guided, only its format being predetermined. There are very large variations in their numbers within an academic department, and in the position they hold there. In some universities and polytechnics, PhD students form a substantial group within their own department, and are seen as respected department members. In other cases, they constitute only a small handful, remaining isolated and marginalised. Nor is there any uniformity in the relation of their research to other departmental work. Sometimes a PhD project forms one part of a larger ongoing investigation directed by an established member of staff. The student in this situation is likely to work as, in some sense, part of a team, and may well be funded. More usually, projects are individually conceived, the research being carried solely by the student concerned. Those registered for PhDs also vary greatly in terms of their employment and economic circumstances. While some are funded and study full-time, many more fund themselves, sometimes at the cost of financial hardship, and struggle to fit their studies into lives busy with work and family responsibilities.

When PhD students are the focus of public concern, as is certainly the case at present, this wide variety tends to be ignored, and a single prototype

1

is taken to constitute the whole group. The doctoral student is defined as full-time and funded, working on the project for perhaps three or at most four years. Such a person is typically young, having often been recruited straight from completing a Masters course in the department; and concomitantly the PhD project will probably represent a further extension of the Masters dissertation. In reality, the average doctoral student is very unlike this picture, not only in being self-funded and part-time but in often being a mature person who, after a long gap, returns to higher education in their thirties, forties or even fifties, and may take many years to complete their project.

If the prototype PhD student is in fact so unrepresentative, why does this picture continue to govern reports and working papers on doctoral studies? The reason almost certainly lies in the parlous economic state in which academic insttutions currently find themselves. Given the major cut-backs of funding and the often extreme financial stringency to which they are subject, universities and polytechnics have necessarily become concerned about any apparently 'unprofitable' areas of their work. In this perspective, questions about research loom large. Funded research contributes to the official credit-worthiness of an institution; and it is new graduates who are most likely to attract research funds. However, the ESRC, the major funding body for the human sciences, now operates a sanctions policy against institutions with what are defined as 'low rates of completion'. It is these 'low rates of completion' which have become the focus of current concern, and which have been taken by nearly all writers to constitute 'the PhD problem'.

The established consensus that PhD students in the social sciences have a poor record in terms of completion is based on an enquiry, set up by the ESRC and carried out by the Winfield Task Force, which produced its report in 1987 (Winfield, 1987). Examining PhD submission among ESRC-funded students over a five year period, these investigators reported that within a three-year period 4% had completed, within four years the figure being 14%, and within five years, 25%. Given that submission after five years was defined as failure, these statistics did indeed look damning. And it is from this starting point that recent studies have worked. Alarmed by these 'low completion rates', a wide variety of bodies has commissioned working parties and research teams. All tend to begin from the same assumption, and to see solutions in the same terms.

Across the various reports and working papers, from the British Psychological Society to the Committee of Vice Chancellors and Principals, there is remarkable unanimity as to the ways in which PhD work needs to be reorganised. If PhD students are to be helped to complete their projects, it is argued, they need far more training in research methods. The Winfield Task Force (Young, McRae, Fogarty, 1987) itself recommended that projects should be structured, like the American model, as formal doctoral programmes. These programmes would entail a substantial taught element, and would cover both substance — the field at issue — and method — the techniques to be mastered. In another study, Phillips and Pugh (1987) suggest that no student should proceed to project work without having first gone through a formal induction programme, and acquired a comprehensive knowledge of research methodology and techniques of analysis. Wilson (1987) goes still further. There should, he believes, be a shift to mixed PhD courses, with no more than 50% representing original research; the remaining 50% would be taken up by formal teaching, to be assessed by written papers and examinations.

Advice such as this is increasingly being put into practice. The development of structured training methods is being funded by the ESRC, which also supports a number of one-year doctoral programmes. Some universities have begun to incorporate research methods courses within their requirements for PhD work. And given the economic pressures in higher education, the need to secure funding and the general consensus that more training is the answer to PhD problems, these trends are likely to continue. Yet the assumptions which underlie this formulation of PhD problems may itself be ill-founded.

The idea that four, or maximally five, years is the outside limit for the completion of a doctoral project is not actually based on any research evidence. Many part-time and some full-time students take longer than this, but nevertheless complete their work successfully. Among their supervisors, there is often a sense that work over a lengthy period may result in something of exceptional quality. Cox (1988), who interviewed academic staff about this question, found that many felt the official time scale to be arbitrary; some referred to students who had produced valuable studies after seven, eight and even nine years. It may also be, as Cox suggests, that a short time limit can deter students from taking on any but 'safe' projects and that work which is riskier but might offer rarer kinds of knowledge, could go by the board. In this sense a narrow time scale can mean a narrow scope. This narrowing would also, perhaps, inevitably be the effect of a doctoral programme which adds in a training element at the expense of original work.

What do PhD students themselves think of the addition of a training element to their work? Such evidence as there is suggests that those who are actually engaged in doctoral work see taught courses on research literature or methodology as an irrelevance. The Winfield Task Force, while concluding in favour of such courses, noted that the PhD students whom they interviewed took an opposite view, seeing little value in them. Similarly Wilson (1987), though advocating formal training, conceded that students generally perceive such training as 'useless'. In his view, students' conceptions of their theses are unduly narrow, and it will be necessary, therefore, to change these conceptions, together with their expectations of what their doctoral studies should involve. Surely there is something strange in this argument. PhD work, as it is generally understood, demands the highest level

3

of autonomous critical reflection. Should the views of those selected for such work be given such very short shrift?

If PhD students typically find taught research courses irrelevant, this does not mean that they have no concern with published research literature or research methodology. The huge success of the annual research workshops run by Burgess at Warwick University (1979 and 1982) bears witness to the vitality of this interest among those engaged in doctoral work. But the nature of these workshops is essentially different from that of a generic taught course. The students who attend do so from their own choice and at an appropriate phase of their own projects. They do not come as an uninformed and uninvolved audience needing to be taught the rules of the research process. Their engagement is an active one, arising from the real, particular and urgent questions thrown up by the research in which they are personally involved. Doctoral studies are inherently difficult and demanding. But the strategies set up to aid them must, if they are to be effective, be firmly grounded in the needs and perceptions of students themselves. Of all levels of education, the organising of this kind of work has surely to be attentive to and respectful of the experience of those who actually undertake it. As yet, no answers have been found to the widespread and well-documented problems of failure, drop-out and low morale amongst PhD students. This is perhaps partly because the solutions typically adopted — most notably those of training — have cavalierly disregarded what such students actually say they need. At a time when these problems, and their possible resolution, are at the forefront of academic concern, it seems vital to listen to the voices of PhD students themselves, speaking about the meaning which this undertaking has for them. This is the goal of this book. By drawing on the experiential accounts of ten students, it sets out to offer first-hand evidence about the PhD experience.

As in any other group of people, the ten contributors to this book are highly diverse: in personal background, research topic, style and general orientation. All, however, have been members of an ongoing group for at least the last three years. Three, having completed their doctorates, remain group members; for the other seven, their projects are as yet incomplete. It is their continuing group membership which has made possible the formulation of this book. Over the years, mutual and collective concerns have evolved out of shared experience. Certain major themes have, in these concerns, seemed crucial to the PhD venture; and it is these themes which govern the structuring of the book.

This group of students also has a common denominator in their supervisor. In this capacity — a capacity which I greatly value — I have, over the years, achieved a 'success' rate well above the usual one. This success does not arise from the operating of some research factory: conducting a large project from which slices get carved off for students. Nor do I function as a guru: proclaiming a total commitment to one theoretical position, to which students must loyally bind themselves. My relative success is simply due, it seems, to the view I hold of PhD work: a view of research as a process, rather than as merely a product. It is this view which informs my demands and expectations and guides my way of supervising. The first two chapters of the book, making up Part One, are an exposition of this view, which forms a shared context within which the ten students experience their work.

The account then goes on in Part Two to introduce the students: the dramatis personae whose comments represent the essential substance of the book. The form of this introduction, ultimately favoured by all those involved, is that of ten pen portraits — my own attempt at a personal sketch of each student in turn. In the main body of the book, five chapters trace particular themes through illustrative extracts from the jotted notes and written expositions which the students offered towards the book. In quoting from these writings, I have altered nothing. Finally comes the epilogue: a brief account of my own experience as a PhD student and over many years as a supervisor.

Part One

Part One

Chapter One

The Character of PhD Research

What qualities in practice entitle a researcher to the award of PhD? The regulations of polytechnics and universities tend to share certain common denominators, setting out what seem to be clear criteria. A PhD thesis must show originality on the one hand and it must make a contribution to knowledge on the other. Originality may be defined further as the discovery of new facts, or the integration of previously diverse ideas. These definitions seem, at first sight, straightforward and unproblematic. Yet, in practice, they often prove ambiguous and slippery. For instance, the academic staff interviewed in a study by Young and others (1987) expressed a general sense of the vagueness of the standards and expectations applying to PhD examining.

Yet if the role of PhD examiner is ill-defined, it is also undoubtedly a demanding one, not something to be lightly undertaken. It is the best theses which make the largest call upon personal resources of time, of thought, of imagination. Such theses, for their examiners, entail a prolonged, necessarily difficult journey, a sustained dwelling within an unfamiliar personal terrain. In the course of this journey, quite unknown ground may be covered, while more familiar scenes may be viewed from entirely new angles. The vistas offered can be alien, both to established views and to one's personal ways of seeing and experiencing. Yet as a reader, one is carried along by the confidence and conviction of the writer; the guide, the pioneer within this new landscape, moves about in it with a sense of authority. In the final analysis, it is this authority, this authorship, which constitutes the touchstone of PhD work.

Defining PhD research in terms of authorship carries certain implications which stand in contrast with the way such work is usually seen. One of these implications concerns the personal, rather than impersonal, character of such work. Authorship entails, in some sense, an ownership of what is being

9

offered. Against the long tradition of viewing scientific knowledge as impersonal, neutral and detached from individuals, this position demands an acknowledgement of the deeply personal roots of the research process, and the preparedness on the student's part to own the concern, directions and meanings which guide it. Taking authorship seriously also entails seeing a research project not as a pre-set, standard sequence of activity but as a creative process, involving its own prolonged, complicated and unpredictable course. As in any creative endeavour, the work of research is transformative — of the researcher as of the work itself. What ultimately emerges in the course of work could not have been foreseen at its beginning. And this is not just a matter of discovering 'facts' which were previously unexpected. Through the creation of meaning which constitutes real research, there comes about a wholly different character in the work, a new visioning of the topic at issue.

PhD projects are sometimes described as a kind of apprenticeship, whereby the student, through carefully applying certain standard scientific procedures to a particular topic, learns how to do research. But being an author necessarily means creating, and the intellectual qualities it calls for are those of imaginative boldness, not slavish obedience to given forms. If PhD students are to write with authority, they must be prepared to think for themselves, to find the courage and the vision to construct their own personal meanings.

If authorship is the touchstone of research, it must entail these three crucial features. A PhD is essentially a personal rather than impersonal undertaking. Like any creative endeavour, it involves its own prolonged and complicated course of development and demands of its students qualities of intellectual boldness and imagination. This perspective is, it seems, totally at variance with the 'training' view of such research. The practices which it calls for in the conduct of PhD projects stand in marked contrast to those entailed by the belief that research can be trained. These differences can be traced from the very beginning of the project.

Before embarking on any project, a student must first register in an academic department. Very different notions of suitability for research work follow from the two viewpoints: that which emphasises authorship and that which emphasises training. It is the second which for the most part governs current practice. In such practice, two criteria tend to operate. First, the candidate's academic record is taken into account, an upper second honours degree being generally seen as a minimum qualification. There is in fact, as Cox (1988) points out, a lack of correlation between undergraduate and postgraduate performance, and this should, at the least, put a question mark over this kind of selection criterion. Certainly it looks irrelevant if research is defined in authorship terms. The ability to absorb received academic ideas, essentially tested by first degree work, may be at a tangent, or even inimical, to the divergent thinking demanded by research. But the linking of the two is quite logical where the crucial element of a PhD is defined as an adequate knowledge of existing research formats.

The second kind of criterion has to do with the proposed project itself. Two aspects are generally emphasised: familiarity with published work on the topic, and knowledge of, if not actually expertise in, a variety of standard research designs and procedures of enquiry and analysis. Drawing on both spheres, the candidate is expected to present a provisional design for the work proposed and show how it relates to previous work. The design should, ideally, specify the research question, the procedures for investigating it, the methods of analysing the results obtained, and the built-in checks against error and bias. A recent advocate of this way of selecting research students is Rudd (1985), who insists that no candidate should be accepted until he or she has completed a thorough literature search and can present a detailed and carefully thought out research proposal.

This approach is standard practice in many university and polytechnic departments. Providing that the candidate appears reasonably conversant with published literature and offers an apparently viable research design — and assuming there is a member of staff available for supervision with a corresponding interest and knowledge — he or she is likely to be accepted. All this seems, on the face of it, unexceptionable. Yet given the view of research adopted here, this initial processing of a potential project appears disastrous. By establishing at the earliest possible stage the broad shape to be given to the undertaking, it cuts short the whole creative process which should define research work. At the very time when the crucial issue itself is likely to be unclear, let alone the form which its investigation might most fruitfully take — at this very moment, everything is pre-empted. Instead of keeping things maximally open, students are required to cast their confused and tentative ideas into a cut-and-dried format. In this way, the work to be done becomes prematurely crystallised. The unwitting effect is likely to be the precluding of possibilities for genuinely creative thinking.

Practices such as these do, of course, arise from a view of research which places paramount importance on the carrying out of certain standard investigatory procedures. In this view, scientific knowledge may be acquired only through the use of established methods of enquiry, the logic of which is considered to allow generalisation. If selection panels typically require candidates to demonstrate their acquaintance with social survey methods, with control groups or double- blind assessments, with bell-shaped distribution curves or the statistical meaning of regression — this is because their potential supervisors see these features as necessary guarantees that the research will be scientifically conducted. Outside the confines of standard designs and measures, it is believed, research could only become chaotic, sloppy, or self-indulgent; any conclusion drawn would represent merely the outcome of chance or of wishful thinking. On this logic, it is only the scrupulous following through of well-established and thoroughly tested procedures which ensures that proper evidence, properly analysed, is adduced to the issue under investigation.

One aspect of this heavy emphasis on research methods is the minimal attention it accords to research questions. It is, of course, a truism that answers can only be as good as the questions to which they are addressed. In research, it is the nature of the issue posed which governs the quality of the work's outcomes. The irrelevance of so much published research in the social sciences, testified by the huge number of unread volumes in academic libraries, is perhaps the clearest demonstration of the humanly irrelevant questions which have guided the work involved. According to the half-flippant categorisation of Rowan Wilson (1968), questions in research are typically of three kinds: Bandwagon, No Stone Unturned, and Fancy That.

The disregard in conventional practice of the significance of research questions is likely merely to perpetuate the proliferation of such ultimately fruitless research. For the posing, in research on human beings, of questions which avoid confusion and transcend the obvious or the trivial, does in fact involve a lengthy process and represents a difficult achievement. Questions that are worth asking must link in to fundamental aspects of the cultural taken-for-granted — the network of assumptions about ourselves and others that operate in the way we go about our lives. But actually to get this at assumptive network means achieving some grasp of what, though crucial, is typically intuitive and inexplicit — Polanyi's tacit knowledge. This is no simple matter. Any research question, in raising one issue, necessarily sets up what is not at issue, what is taken for granted. And the validity and centrality of these taken-for-granted assumptions are as important, for the fertility of any research project, as what is explicitly set at issue.

For doctoral students the very early definition of research questions does not merely pre-empt the outcome of what should entail a long creative process. It also acts totally to obscure the inescapably personal and personal-social character of all questions. A basic aspect of the traditional view of research is, of course, its separation of what is known from the one who knows. The body of scientific knowledge is regarded as having entirely independent standing — as out there, equally accessible and equally valid for all who choose to consult it. Yet as Heisenberg reminds us, we do not know nature, but only 'nature exposed to our methods of questioning'. And knowledge of any kind arises out of the enquiries of particular human beings, who have particular questions, purposes, expectations, assumptions and hopes. The grounding of scientific knowledge within the human concerns, social positions and vested interests of particular social groupings goes unnoticed, so often, because those who make recourse to it typically share the same concerns, the same positions, the same interests. This kind of knowledge therefore comes to be seen as common knowledge, free-standing, universal, and beyond dispute.

When would-be research students are invited to present proposals to an academic selection panel, the usual expectation is that they will have derived their research questions from existing published work within the area. 'So-and-So found such-and-such. I thought I would extend his work to a younger age range/different cultural groups.' 'Such-and Such a measure is generally agreed to have problems. I should like to test out some different formats.' Such formulations will probably be seen as basically satisfactory; they show an awareness of the research consensus, and follow up 'the' questions — that is, the standard questions that previous researchers would agree to be important. How different 'the' questions would look if they were offered by the social groupings who are to act as the research subjects! In the perspectives of people outside the narrow academic community, what can be assumed, what matters, what urgently needs asking may be a world away from what is taken for granted by those who publish research findings about these people. And the issues posed by mature doctoral candidates are, because of their own life experience, often grounded in the experience of just this kind of constituency.

Because research questions are rooted in the personal and personal-social situation of those who pose them, beginning students need to devote a large proportion of time, concern, creative feeling and imaginative thought to the formulating of a central issue. There can be no quick and thoughtless opting for some ready-made, second-hand question taken from the literature, with all that such a question begs about the area concerned. The first, long and difficult phase of a research project involves developing the fullest, deepest sense possible of the sphere at issue. This is not achieved simply by a thorough perusal of published work about the topic; indeed such work, by its crystallisation of meaning along particular lines, can often hinder the development of new understanding. Part of this phase necessitates a personal immersion within the area concerned, so that it becomes known from the inside and experienced, as nearly as possible, in the terms of those who actually live it. Only after this personal immersion can issues begin to be formulated. And at this stage, it is important to recognise that these issues are inescapably, and rightly, personal.

Traditionally scientific activity has no place for what is personal. Personal involvement is seen as suspect, as undermining the detachment and neutrality essential for science. Yet in the end, it is the passionate caring of a researcher which both sustains the research undertaking and gives the outcomes their meaning and vitality. So far from undermining research work, personal commitment to it ensures its quality; it is the lack of such commitment which leads to short cuts, dishonesty or the reduction of work to a ritualistic exercise. A published psychological research report on morality serves to illustrate how this may happen. The design of the research entailed misinforming the subjects as to the purpose of the tasks they were invited to do and secretly installing a one-way observation mirror to record how they behaved. Such a way of conducting research can occur only if the research question means absolutely nothing to the researcher personally. Claiming a serious interest in morality, yet failing to consider the morality of one's own procedures, one's own relations with subjects, ignoring the fact that the research question is equally implicated in one's investigative behaviour — this is possible only for those who have totally divorced themselves and their personal understandings from what they are doing in the name of psychological research. The outcome of such work is, inevitably, the sort of insulting and wholly unenlightening study of which there are all too many examples in the literature.

The personal character of good research means that the whole venture is suffused with feeling. The vague but real excitement felt in beginning one's own research is something to be taken seriously, valued, nurtured. All too often, this sense of excitement quickly evaporates in the process of hardening up the research design. Translating as yet inchoate ideas into ready-made, second-hand question and methods may make for a clear, even an apparently impressive project, but it is likely to leave a sense of inward flatness, dreariness and disappointment.

In the research process, a confused sense of the personal significance of a research topic may, if protected, eventually develop into the formulation of a unique research question which has deep personal roots. This process entails a mulling over of intuitive kinds of understanding, in the light of a developing appreciation of other relevant perspectives and understandings. Out of this difficult kind of thinking may emerge a definite issue which is uniquely one's own, which embodies deep personal conviction, carries personally held values, yet honestly puts into question other aspects which are of real personal consequence. The posing of research questions represents, essentially, the taking up of a particular stance towards that part of the human world. Only if that stance is consonant with one's own most characteristic, most deeply felt positions towards life, will the research question hold inner conviction and carry the wealth of personal implication which alone makes it worth asking.

If the formulation of the issue defining any research question involves a lengthy and difficult process, the translating of that question into a real-life enquiry is perhaps no less demanding. Unfortunately students often find that this phase of research is again grossly truncated. To take seriously any research question should mean recognising that the decision as to how to operationalise it is nothing if not problematic. For the relation between an issue and any of the myriad ways of investigating it is highly complex. How a question is to be posed, what kind of evidence will be relevant, how such evidence should be gathered, examined, considered — all this requires the lengthiest and the most careful deliberation and is not to be resolved merely by reaching for the nearest hand-me-down research design. In human enquiries, the hasty opting for certain methods merely on grounds of viability is likely to be particularly disastrous. The subjects in social science research are human beings; and human beings have values, meanings, purposes of their own. The psychological perspectives of subjects, whether similar to those of each other or of the researcher, can certainly not be ignored. Neither can the fact that encounters between investigators and their subjects are social situations between people, no less complicated than other social situations between people. It is inescapable that human beings do not always agree about what a thing means, nor about what is evidence of something; and this surely matters as much in making judgments as to the significance of the behaviour or experience of subjects, as it does in communicating to the academic community what any research findings may mean. All this adds up, at the very least, to the fact that setting up honest and valid human enquiries is complex and difficult and that these problems are inherent in research, not to be side-stepped by the adopting of standardised questionnaires or the application of statistical tests of chance.

Conventional expectations and guidance of PhD research, which emphasise the products rather than the process of such work, entail the heaviest pressure on students to arrive quickly at a final structuring of the project, so that the 'real work' — the gathering of data — can begin. Because the essentially creative, authoring character of research goes unrecognised in such practice, PhD students are likely to feel a need to hasten on to the fieldwork stage. If they have undergone the task during selection procedures of presenting their proposal as a fully worked out design, this is liable to produce its own problems. As with all such premature shapings, the plan presented publicly has a way of sticking. Once a format has been constructed, it is hard to break things open again and free oneself, even privately, from its structure.

But even beyond the assumptions and practices of traditional research guidance, students themselves are apt, usually, to face strong inner pressures. It is the creative character of PhD research which, while constituting its essential value, also entails the most arduous, lonely, and challenging work. Faced with the need to forge one's own personal direction — a long, chaotic, often seemingly fruitless inner struggle, in which no one else can help and for which there is no guaranteed outcome — the temptation to cut the whole thing short can be very great. The eagerness to start quickly on fieldwork, the feeling that only then will research really be being 'done', is hardly surprising. During the hardest, most testing phases of creative work, there is nothing to show, no account to offer sceptical friends of what the whole thing means, unlike the real-life data, the visible material, which so often impresses others and seems to confirm the doing of a worthwhile activity. Yet such data, gathered for its own sake and not as material embedded within a deeply thought-out personal framework, will in the end represent merely so many words, unread by others, lacking any implication for human life.

It is perhaps, in the last analysis, these inner factors which make the doing of meaningful research most difficult. Taking authorship of one's own project entails going profoundly against the grain of most academic activity. To acknowledge in one's own work deeply personal directions and concerns — this is a daunting and a daring thing to do. It requires an act of inner assertion, a claim to own something of a topic which is widely seen to belong

15

not to individual persons but to the whole scientific community — to the published literature, the big names. To make such a claim demands ceasing to hide behind the skirts of others, fearful of making any statement, any judgment, that cannot be supported by a reference to published work. As Becker (1986) puts it, students have somehow to stop being 'terrorised by the literature'. This does not, of course, means an arrogant dismissal of the thinking and the work which others have offered towards the topic in question. But the ideas of others — in early reading, in reflection following fieldwork, in written discussion of relevant literature — need to be considered not naively or deferentially, but from the position of one's own thought-out personal stance towards the issues involved. If this can be achieved and material adduced which has crucial bearing upon this stance, then the project will possess real authority. It is a major task, which calls above all for qualities of courage and intellectual boldness.

How is this large goal brought about and why, so often, do people fail to achieve it? Two opposing views of PhD work need to be thought about by anyone who embarks on this kind of study. Their differences go far beyond those merely of emphasis: of a greater or lesser knowledge of methodology. For ultimately, they entail contrasting and irreconcilable definitions of enquiry, of knowledge and of learning.

A 'training' view of PhD research — at least in its hardest form — rests in the last analysis on the assumption that such work is a matter of the proper application of certain standard methods of enquiry. In this, the major parameters are essentially given. There is a right timescale, a right sequence, proper kinds of question, correct methods of investigation and analysis. Scientific enquiry, though it is seen as technically complex and difficult, is not viewed as inherently problematic for those who undertake it.

Underlying this perspective on enquiry is a definition of knowledge in essentially positivistic terms. What a student is to be offered by way of training is a set of free-standing techniques whose universal viability is not in question. Yet, as several writers have suggested, the technical is never purely that. Research techniques are inextricably entangled, for instance, with local cultures and ideologies. Murray (1988) argues that within academic disciplines, as well as academic institutions, there are built-in conflicts of methodology; he instances the status of survey techniques as between empirical and critical sociologists. In the view of Wakeford (1981), a long-term critic of graduate courses in methodology, it is their decontextualising of research processes which is their most basic flaw. As he points out, the whole social, economic and political context within which research takes place goes altogether unexamined in such courses.

A view of research knowledge as something to be acquired by training must ultimately reduce it to specific skills relating to already defined problems. But what is surely demanded in research is the development of understanding — an understanding which is able to grasp the conceptual underpinnings, the values, the human stance that lie within particular ways of doing social science research. This is an understanding which essentially questions and challenges accepted ways of defining issues and investigating them, which has to be intellectually independent rather than merely conforming. For if research is to develop our appreciation of social organisations and ways of functioning as human beings, it needs to do more than reproduce existing meanings; researchers have to evolve their own structures of meaning. As Cox (1988) suggests in his extended consideration of research training, it is education rather than training which PhD students most essentially need.

In its fullest sense, education has always connoted a more than narrowly cognitive process. The personal and emotional character which is so often left out of account in considering PhD work needs, surely, to feature largely in the processes through which such work comes to develop. For research is personally transforming; and the development which it entails has ramifications within personal identity. The scheme which Perry (1970) proposes in defining mature kinds of learning seems relevant here. Perry suggests four levels. In the first, 'dualistic' stage, one is likely to be dominated by the idea that right answers must be found and wrong ones rejected. Next, at the relativistic stage, there is an awareness of the multiplicity of possible approaches to the question. Following on from this comes the stage of commitment; accepting the need for a definite act of commitment to a specific stance towards the issue. Only at the final, 'dynamic commitment' phase, does one realise that this commitment demands personal kinds of change and development.

For those who hope to achieve this kind of learning through a PhD project, a very special kind of education is required. It is not didactic teaching which is needed, but support in learning from personal engagement in the research. This entails learning by doing: what Schon (1987) defines as reflecting-in-action. As Diana Laurillard (1987) suggests, this kind of education lies a world away from transmission of information or skills. Reflecting on one's own activities enables one to learn directly rather than merely receiving from a teacher. The relation with tutors has to be that of open communication, in which knowledge is a commodity between tutor and student. Such a relation, Laurillard believes, puts the student into a position of ultimate control.

An emphasis on the authorial character of PhD work, in contrast with an emphasis on the need for training, carries, it is evident, some basic implications about its manner of supervising. As Cox and his colleagues point out (Cox et al, 1988), the relationship between student and supervisor is at the heart of doctoral work, yet little is known about it. No research has been done, for instance, on such basic aspects as frequency, extent or content of supervisory meetings. It is the whole question of supervision which forms the focus of the next chapter.

18

Chapter Two

PhD Supervision

'That PhD student of mine, what a bind she is. The whole term gone, and she's brought nothing. I'm just going to have to chase her yet again'. On her side the student is no less troubled. 'I hope to goodness I don't meet my supervisor in the library today. He's sure to ask what I've been doing, and I've got absolutely nothing to show him.'

Asked what it is that PhD supervision is actually for, both sides in the relationship would, typically, lay the heaviest emphasis on chasing students. Supervising, it is generally assumed, means above all keeping the student up to the mark — making sure, by gentle persuasion or by tough talking, that the research project gets started, is carried through and is finally written up. In this, the meeting of deadlines is seen as crucial; it is up to the supervisor to see that time is not wasted. If the student is to complete within the recognised number of years, there must be no delay in any of the stages involved. Within a few months of registration, relevant literature should have been read and the research design established. Next, pilot work needs to be done, following which the main fieldwork should be carried out. Then the results should be exhaustively analysed and conclusions drawn. Nor can there be any sitting back until the final stage, writing up the work to produce a final draft, is complete. The supervisor's most essential role in all this is that of constantly reminding, prompting, chasing.

This delineation of the main supervisory function is, in conventional practice, endorsed by those involved in any aspect of PhD work, and it is usually followed conscientiously and effortfully by those who take on supervision. Yet supervising PhDs seems, all too often, to be experienced as a thankless task and one which may frequently prove ultimately unsuccessful. Despite the goodwill and effort of most supervisors, students often feel unhappy: as Cox and others (1988) report, nearly a quarter of those interviewed were dissatisfied with the supervision they received. And within the approach adopted here, this is unsurprising. Defining the supervisor as a chaser is fundamentally misguided, and potential projects treated in this way are all too likely to be killed off.

If PhD supervision is traditionally seen as largely a matter of chasing up students, this derives from a view of research as the application of standard scientific procedures to a given question. Such a view carries certain implications about how the work should, ideally, proceed. Many of these implications have to do with the ordering of research. Essentially, this is seen as standard. No matter what their sphere, all projects are reviewed as entailing the same basic schedule, the same stages of work, to be gone through in the same order: the perusal of literature, the choice of research design, the pilot work, the main fieldwork, the analysis, the conclusion, the write-up. And as someone familiar with this schedule through reading, original research and supervising other projects, the PhD supervisor seems to constitute the obvious guide and regulator of the student's progress.

Yet over and over again, that progress turns out, to be unaccountably problematic. Somehow the student, so eager, so enthusiastic in the early stages, seems unable to deliver the product itself — the evidence of reading, of decisions as to methodology, of the actual application of scientific measures to the research population. Obtaining anything in writing from this student seems like getting blood from a stone. Worse still, all the initial enthusiasm seems to have ebbed away. The supervisory role has inexplicably been transformed from one of welcomed interest to one of dreaded, guilt-inducing bullying.

The vision of research offered here calls for a very different conception of supervision. If PhD work is viewed as a process rather than a product, then what matters most is the private thinking, the feeling and imagining, the mulling over of contradiction, possibility and implication, which constitutes the real stuff of original research. Important thought the visible outcomes may be — the translation of personal questions, of concerns and insights into the format of real-life enquiry — ultimately these outcomes are less significant than the thinking that lies behind them and which, in the end, renders them humanly weighty and meaningful, rather than trivial. This view emphasises not the traditional stages of research as such but the work that goes on between them and the preparedness to make each stage a problem to be personally thought out, rather than a ready-made exercise to be obediently followed. To take seriously, as PhD supervisor, the creative nature of PhD research, with all the difficult personal demands it must inevitably make on its students, means undertaking a very different kind of role and responsibility from the one conventionally adopted. The quality that supervision needs above all to offer is that of personal support.

In traditional thinking, research is seen as an impersonal venture in which the contaminating effects of individual feeling and circumstances are scrupulously eliminated by the use of proper scientific methods. Impersonality is seen as defining the character not just of the researcher's conduct but also of the various relationships which research involves. Having a personal interest in research is often viewed with suspicion, as putting a question mark over the necessary detachment with which the topic should be approached. Relating personally to those who act as subjects in the work would, almost universally, be frowned on. And relations between students and their supervisors are also conventionally seen as needing to keep a certain distance. Though offering much goodwill, kindness and encouragement, a supervisor, in the usual academic view, must avoid too close a personal involvement with a research student or risk losing the capacity to be properly, scientifically critical.

What is suggested here is not merely that real research is indelibly personal but that its personal character, thoughtfully worked through and honestly set at issue, represents its greatest strength. This has implications for supervision. Agreeing to supervise a project means undertaking to work in close collaboration with someone who is embarking on a journey within themselves — a journey which may at times be profoundly exciting but which will also certainly be difficult, risky and painful. Accompanying someone on such a journey entails a very personal, often very intimate, kind of communication. A successful supervisory relationship, so far from being merely a matter of scientific expertise and academic interest in the topic, depends crucially on mutual sympathy and trust and on a personal resonance on the part of the supervisor, to the student's sense of meaning and excitement.

These considerations operate from the very beginning of PhD supervision. Supervisor-student partnerships need to be set up on the basis of a potential, felt on both sides, for a quite intimate kind of working together. By the same token, close supervision cannot fruitfully be duplicated. Research focuses and directions acknowledged and given meaning within one relational context are liable to become diffused, fragmented and changed in another, where the student has more than one supervisor.

Such a position is at variance with established practice and the direction of most current formulations of supervisory requirements. In his study of postgraduate failure, for example, Rudd (1985) suggests that inadequate supervision is a major cause. In his view, to rely on the knowledge and commitment of a single supervisor is dangerous and he advocates the setting up of a supervisory committee. Similarly Phillips and Pugh (1987) argue that one person could not hope to offer the required range of academic expertise needed in PhD supervision. These writers, like many of those who act as supervisors, essentially view the supervisory function in terms of knowledgeability rather than relationship. In keeping with this view, they assume a one-way basis for setting up supervisory partnerships. The student gets selected by the supervisor. Yet trust, sympathy and mutual resonance are not merely luxuries or by-products: they represent the essential basis of successful supervisory relationships. If these qualities are not reciprocally felt, students will not have access to the encouragement and support that are vital in doctoral work.

When students begin to embark on the project they have planned, one of their most difficult tasks is to establish their own way of working. In this, the personal character of supervision is often crucial. Although, in conventional thinking, the progress of any piece of research is essentially standard, in fact every approach to research is idiosyncratic. There can be no universally viable timetable, no generalisable order of work, no uniform number of hours per day, no standard mechanism for engaging or disengaging with the project. Everyone has to find within themselves ways of working on their own piece of research which both fit with the rest of their lives and — at least at times — bring about a sense of progress. All this is very difficult. The creative process is itself notoriously capricious. Most PhD students, additionally, have both work and family or domestic responsibilities, leaving only limited time and energies available for research. In the case of many women students in particular, there are often inner barriers against a confident claim to the right to spend time on personal work. Yet given that, for most students, their PhD project represents their first experience of independent research. It is at this stage that a personally viable mode of work needs to be discovered.

In conventional wisdom, one of the supervisor's responsibilities is to channel the student into the proper, standard way of working, with its overall schedule, its built-in order of tasks, each with its own timing and modes of operation. Though in the short term such guidance and direction may come as a relief to someone floundering in uncertainties, in the end it can only prove destructive. Ways of working cannot be imposed from without; they have to be created, individually and personally. As Murray (1988) argues, imposing methodologies on PhD work can be disastrous: in his view, PhD projects often founder because students are pushed into using methods which do not personally suit them. And from the pioneering work of Gough and Woodworth (1960) it is clear that there is a very wide diversity of ways of doing research. Among professional research scientists they identified no less than eight stylistic variations: they labelled these zealot, initiator, diagnostician, scholar, artifact, aestheticist, methodologist and independent. In the difficult task of evolving a personal way of working, a supervisor who is delicately attuned to the student can be of real help. One aspect of a personal, rather than impersonal, supervisory relationship is that it entails an acknowledgement of the student as a person in the round. Discussion of the work includes a recognition of the life situation of which the research project is part. Non-academic matters do not have to be discarded at the office door; supervisor and student can together mull over the absence of a room at home to work in, the demands of a young child, or the fact that ideas seem to come only at impossible moments and never when research time has been set aside.

What often makes this task more difficult still is that students themselves may have assimilated the prevailing ethos about 'right' ways of doing research. Many departments adopt certain practices intended to ensure that PhD students do not drop out and that they complete their projects within a specified period. Regular reminders about the passing of time and the concomitant need to show evidence of work done, typically act to induce a sense of personal urgency, even panic. Being required to present the project to a seminar of postgraduates often leads to feelings of near-desperation, and a conviction that everyone else has achieved personally unattainable levels of progress. In this situation, students frequently impose on themselves the heaviest moral strictures, making impossible self-demands which will inhibit rather than facilitate their work. So far from needing to act as chaser, a supervisor in these circumstances needs to counter the student's own excessive, potentially destructive self-chasing. For someone in this state of mind, it is reassuring to hear of the variety of time scales and modes of work which others have successfully used. More importantly still, a supervisor who is personally attuned to the student's vital concerns and feelings can often draw upon these to break the vicious circle of blocked work and self-reproach and act as a reminder of abiding commitments, and intentions that are still valid.

This perspective does, necessarily, accord motivational power to PhD students rather than to their supervisors. Where, traditionally, it is the supervisor who is seen as needing to keep the student up to scratch — to use both stick and carrot to prevent a natural tendency to fall by the wayside — in the view offered here, it is the student's own passionate commitment to the project which, if anything, will carry it through. As Phillips and Pugh (1987) have argued, in the course of PhD work students become their own independent critics, well able to evaluate their own efforts and to set their own standards both of quality and of productivity. This does not make supervisors redundant; rather it defines their role as one of responsiveness and aliveness to the underlying commitment — especially at times when students themselves lose their sense of it.

One implication of this position has to do with a supervisor's relation to the sphere of research with which a project is concerned. In the conventional wisdom, the supervisory capacity of academic staff derives from their expertise: with scientific methodology on the one hand and with the area of research on the other. Familiarity with this sphere through extensive reading, teaching and perhaps original work does, it is assumed, confer the right to act as a guide to a research student. The role is that of mapping the area, delineating the major lines of work within it, defining 'the' issues and concepts, acknowledging the known names, rehearsing the unresolved problems. In all this the supervisor is an expert, the student, as yet, only a novice.

Again, this constitutes a misreading of supervision, because it fails to accommodate any idea that a PhD student comes to adopt a particular, unique stance towards the sphere of research involved. Though research literature is traditionally viewed as neutral and established — a given landscape whose features, once learned, can be unquestionably accepted as real — in fact, any body of 'knowledge' incorporates its own concerns, assumptions and interests. If research is to make any real contribution to human understanding, it must entail a close and deeply thoughtful consideration and questioning of what is implicit in previous work. Since guiding assumptions are by their nature tacit rather than overt, recognising something of them is far from easy and it is often achieved only after the researcher has explored the area in more personal ways. The thorough reviewing of literature may sometimes be better done after rather than before field work. But as against representing an obedient acceptance of 'the story so far', mediated by a supervisor familiar with the field, this aspect of PhD work means establishing a unique personal standpoint from which previous work is consciously considered. When this is achieved, it is the student rather than the supervisor who has become the expert, who can speak with real authority. In the course of this process, other work which has implications for the project is positively devoured; there is no need for a supervisor to lead an ignorant, reluctant student through the field of literature.

In the usual thinking about PhD supervision, supervisors are also seen to represent expertise in the sphere of methodology. At the stage where the student is planning the design of the project —its subject groups, its ways of assessing, the forms of analysis to which results will be subjected—at this stage, it is assumed, supervisors can appropriately offer guidance as to the best choices to be made. In keeping with the traditional perspective on scientific work, this view entirely separates methodology from content and assumes that relations with subjects, approaches to enquiry and ways of interpreting human material can all be considered independently of the particular project involved. Yet, in fact, the translation of an issue into a uniquely relevant format of enquiry constitutes one of the major tasks of research work. It entails the following through of the logic underlying the stance from which the issue has been defined, so that this logic equally informs the position adopted in the whole methodology of the work. Ultimately, means and ends are undistinguishable; and a research project is defined by the approach and methods which it uses, just as crucially as by its declared intentions. All too frequently, these connections are ignored, so that the position explicitly adopted within a piece of research comes to be violated by its methodology. As with all the key stages in research work, the devising of truly appropriate ways of setting up an enquiry is extremely difficult. In this, it helps to have a supervisor whose support derives from a sympathetic appreciation and respect for the deepest levels of meaning involved in the work and whose concern for these meanings helps to hold the balance against temptation to take short cuts.

If the appropriate supervisory role is that of personal support, it is above all the process of imaginative envisaging, of inner dwelling upon meaning, which, in PhD work, needs to be supported. And such support can be offered not only in the close encounters of student and supervisor but also in a wider community of relations, which supervisors can do much to foster. The arrangement of meetings with other students and with staff are, of course, an established part of most supervisory practice. An underlying concern is with counteracting the well-documented sense of loneliness and isolation associated with PhD work. But there is also usually another, more academic motive behind these arrangements. In many departments PhD students are invited (in terms which disallow refusal) to present their ongoing work to an audience of other postgraduates and academic staff. The rationale of these invitations is that such occasions help students to define and sharpen up their ideas, through having to articulate clearly what they are trying to do, and by providing a critical audience, they offer an opportunity to modify inadequacies before it is too late. However, the usual outcomes of this kind of seminar tend to fall far short of the intentions behind them, leaving students feeling, at best, uncomfortably exposed to critical judgment and, at worst, undermined and demoralised.

Group encounters of this kind do, of course, take place within the ambience of a philosophy which defines research as product rather than as process and places emphasis on correctness of standard procedures, as against the capacity to sustain imaginative thought and to evolve a richness of human implication. This is an aspect considered by Schon (1987) who suggests that all too often intellectual competitiveness and mutual point-scoring get disguised as rational academic discourse. Yet groups can, within a different philosophy, be used to nourish and affirm the essentially creative qualities which mark original research. An ongoing group of students who share the same supervisor, meeting regularly, can offer each other vital mutual support. The extent to which this happens is dependent, however, on the expectations conveyed by the supervisor and this means going markedly against the grain of the students' own experience of academic work.

If meetings of PhD students are to avoid the kind of petty and competitive point-scoring which mars so many postgraduate seminars, they need to work to a quite different agenda to the traditional one. What is required is an atmosphere in which, above all, personal concerns and personal feelings can be safely shared. While such communication may be typical of therapeutic groups, it is altogether alien to academic ones. The absence of a traditional agenda — of group members in turn 'presenting' plans, progress, results — is typically felt to be very uncomfortable by students joining this kind of group. Anxiety-producing though it may be, the demand to take part in the usual academic dialogue is at least familiar: you know where you are, whereas this lack of clear structure seems ambiguous and has no guaranteed outcome. Yet in the course of time, abandoning the usual academic rules of talk produces rich rewards. Having no need to divorce yourself from what you are doing, to claim an expertise you do not feel, to pretend progress or offer shame-faced apologies for its absence — the freedom from these pressures allows for a far greater openness, honesty and genuine sharing.

For almost everyone, it comes as a revelation that others too experience blocks, self doubt, periods of despair: so carefully are these universal features of research disguised, whether in seminars or in the literature. The sharing of deep personal concern, of excitement and hope, as well as anxiety and frustration, acts to build close personal bonds between group members, who develop over time real mutual respect and caring. In the isolation and loneliness of original work, the sense of a continuity of group concern can be a vital support.

But group meetings can provide another way of encouraging research, even beyond that of mutual support. Potentially, such meetings represent a forum for the development of very personal kinds of imaginative exploration. If research is to move beyond conventional wisdom, it has to engage with what is as yet intuitive, unarticulated, beyond the level of coherent meaning. This calls for the use of modes, often non-verbal, which contrast markedly with those of academic dialogue. Sometimes, with the prompting and encouragement of a supervisor, PhD students can undertake such work alone. But the context of a small group which has established a sense of mutual trust potentially offers richer opportunities for the development of this kind of intuitive exploration.

This aspect of PhD work — totally neglected in conventional supervisory practice — entails the use of ad hoc kinds of exercise designed to widen the focus of awareness of what is involved in the research. Two such exercises which I recently set up myself will serve to illustrate. The first has to do, broadly, with students' own personal orientations. One reason why it is so often difficult to move forward confidently in research is that there is a vague yet insistent sense of a multitude of contradictory perspectives on the topic. From the shadowy background of the work loom groups of subjects or potential subjects, previous researchers, colleagues, the whole academic world; particular individual figures, too, seem to be looking over the student's shoulder — the supervisor, possible examiners, parents, friends or partners, perhaps a critical teacher from long ago. There appears to be a diversity of conflicting demands and claims, of discrepant interests in the research. Some of these may be relevant and legitimate but others are perhaps more questionable. While they remain obscure presences, felt rather than known, these perspectives cannot be dealt with nor their influence taken into account in defining the research directions.

The exercise I devised was aimed at clarifying this situation and bringing out of the shadows, for members of the PhD group, the people and interests by whom they felt themselves as researchers to be surrounded. It entailed using the technique of group sculpture. Those who chose to take part set up a tableau of the various interests felt to be involved in their own research, using themselves and others in the group as raw material. This exercise offered a way of viewing who was 'there', and how they stood towards the work. It proved, in several cases, to illuminate an obscure but vitally important aspect of the research undertaking.

Another exercise was concerned with a more specific, but equally crucial, feature of human enquiry. If research is to have value, it must reveal as fully and honestly as possible the situation and experience of those who represent its subjects. Any PhD project necessarily calls for an intense and sustained effort by the student to enlarge personal understanding of the group or persons who are its focus. This exercise set out to explore this understanding from an unusual angle and in so doing to develop it further. In groups of three, each student took turns to role play an imaginary member of their own subject group, while the other two students assumed the part of interested questioners. This meant for instance that one person responded as a 13-year-old girl struggling with the stresses of school life, while another spoke from the complicated situation of a mature woman who has recently returned to formal education. This exercise too proved generally fruitful. Actually to enter imaginatively into the experience of research subjects can bring about a very special and intimate understanding which perhaps could never be attained while remaining in the role of a researcher, however sensitive.

The fostering of group support and the use of exploratory group work should form one part of a supervisor's overall responsibility. When it comes to the last phase of PhD work, however, there is no doubt that the individual collaboration between student and supervisor is crucial. Here again, very special qualities of personal support are called for on the part of the supervisor. So far from representing an easy stage — a mere tying of things together after the real work has been done — writing up a PhD project inevitably proves extremely difficult and demanding. This is not just because some vital reference turns out to be indecipherable or because the original tabulation of some material needs to be reworked. More fundamentally, writing up a piece of work demands a reconceptualisation of the whole project. Only through such rethinking can decisions be made as to what should be included and what omitted in the write-up, how to present work carried out within a perspective which has since been abandoned, or what final evaluation should be made of the undertaking. And as Becker (1986) argues, this writing task can only be learned through the doing of it: until students actually become engaged in it, this difficult task remains a mystery. Faced with this major task after years of difficult work, feeling, perhaps, a weariness and a wish to move on, most students, not surprisingly, are tempted to take short cuts at this stage and opt for a quickly written format which does less than justice to their own work.

At this stage, the support of a supervisor can be critical. To find that this person remains intensely interested in the work, to the extent of giving it personal priority over other business, and still insists on its value by refusing to accept facile formulations — this is in the end deeply encouraging to someone struggling with this final difficult phase. The capacity to offer such encouragement proceeds, again, from a very personal appreciation of the student's undertaking. It entails responding to written drafts, not from an impersonal and generalised position with its standard criteria of evaluation,

27

but from an awareness and respect for the uniqueness of what is being offered. If the supervisor needs to be tough towards students' written offerings, this toughness proceeds from a determination that the personal concerns and the personal logic which informed the research itself shall equally govern the ways in which it is presented to its readership. Just as the translation of a deeply thought personal issue into the format of a real-life enquiry requires a unique working-out, so the format of a completed PhD thesis has to be individually, personally created within the philosophy which has guided the research.

There is, perhaps, one final task which should form part of a supervisor's responsibility. This is to help a student who is waiting to be examined to achieve an appropriate orientation towards the examination. Here again, as with every stage in PhD work, there is a tendency to slip into accustomed roles and forget what is essentially involved in this very special kind of undertaking. By the stage of PhD thesis submission, every student has acquired much experience of being an examinee — of being subjected to external assessments and, if not actually being found wanting, of knowing the possibility of failure. The universal posture is a humble one: examinees can only hope to meet the standards which others, not they, have defined. But for a PhD student, the situation is very different. The terrain of judgment is essentially of their own making. As author of a research, the student ultimately defines the terms of discussion and the kinds of criteria which should be brought to bear on the work. Of course this does not mean that in their examination PhD candidates should adopt an arrogance towards the work involved. Of all people, those who have honestly thought through their own research are typically most conscious of its shortcomings. Nor does this stance entail a lack of responsiveness to and appreciation of the perspectives and the criticisms which examiners themselves may suggest. What is called for is a position based on the recognition of what it is that the whole PhD project has involved. Whatever the examination's outcomes, the candidate within it can speak with authority about the research in question.

Part Two

Chapter Three

Introducing the ten students

☐ ANN

My first encounter with Ann was fairly disastrous and nearly put paid to her becoming a research student. For Ann, the experience was one which revived life-long doubts, conflicts and resentments about the status of her own knowledge. She came to see me to talk about the possibility of registering for a research degree in the field of anti-racist education. This field was one in which Ann herself had achieved eminence. Her pioneering work in developing a curriculum for teaching equality at infant level had attracted the attention not merely of other interested head and class teachers and of advisers and inspectors but also of educational broadcasters and writers. As we talked together, the breadth of her first-hand experience and the depth of her anger at social injustice in the lives of children were very clear. Like all beginning students, however, she was necessarily vague as to precisely what issue she hoped to investigate in her research. Trying both to affirm her obvious commitment and to encourage her to explore her ideas further, I suggested that, before actually proceeding to register, she should visit the Institute's Centre for Multicultural Education. To talk with the staff of this Centre would certainly be helpful and Ann might perhaps consider taking a seconded term as a Visiting Associate there.

Ann heard this advice in very different terms to the way it was intended. Not registering the meaning of what I was suggesting, she took me to be side-tracking her research application. For her, this revived long-standing feelings towards academia and 'clever' people: feelings of ignorance and inadequacy together with a sense of rage and rebellion against those in positions of apparent intellectual authority. It seemed that her own real-life understanding of race, class and gender inequality was being dismissed out of hand in favour of some other kind of knowledge which she did not have and which was the possession of people from another world than her own. For Ann this interview merely added to much previous bitter experience; it showed her yet again that working class people were profoundly at a disadvantage in the enlargement of life chances.

Happily, this meeting was not the last between Ann and myself, for she returned to talk more fully about the work she hoped to do and on this occasion we seemed able to avoid bypassing each other. But the reactions which Ann had at our first meeting do arise again from time to time, particularly in the context of group meetings, where the use of a certain kind of language or the assumption of familiarity with the academic world reawaken her sense of angry bewilderment. These feelings relate in very significant ways to the difficult research which she has undertaken. In some sense, they reflect the relation between lived understanding and conceptual knowledge. Ann is herself a practitioner — and an outstanding one at that. Somehow in evolving her research, she needs to make articulate the intuitive basis of her innovative practice.

If energy, resourcefulness and commitment are vital to the carrying through of personal research, Ann's own history makes her well qualified. Leaving school at sixteen, she did not return to education until the age of twenty-seven, by which time her own son was settled at school. Having trained as a teacher, she combined classroom teaching with a whole succession of part-time diplomas and degrees: in-service courses, a diploma in multicultural education, a BEd degree. Rapidly rising to deputy headship, she then took up a headship in an infants' school in East London and after four years the post of head of a primary school, also in East London. While dealing in the classroom and in management with all the problems of an inner-city school — problems of stressed children, of recruiting, retaining and supporting staff at a time of teacher shortage, of poor resources and low morale — throughout in all this, Ann has also been an active partner, mother and daughter. The real fire in the belly which energises her life will, if anything can, enable her to stay with the problems of her own difficult but highly worthwhile project.

☐ CHRIS

My earliest meeting with Chris was the prototype of many future encounters over the years in which we have worked together. He came before a selection panel on which I had been invited to sit, because the repertory grid methodology which he had mentioned in his application lay in my general sphere of interest. Despite goodwill on both sides, the occasion was extremely uncomfortable. Questioned about his PhD proposal, Chris struggled, with obvious carefulness and sincerity, to provide adequate answers. Yet the more he talked, the more elusive seemed his intentions; with every explanation he added, the project became increasingly obscure. He had said that his research was to involve deaf people as his subjects. The staff member with expertise in the deaf proceeded to ask him about this, with gradually evaporating confidence. For it seemed that Chris's interest was not in deafness as such but rather in exploring the situation of deaf people as representing unique locations within a configuration of multiple realities. The deaf were not, he explained, any different in this from hearing people. He confused his questioner still further by remarking that his sample would probably include hearing people also. This did not mean, as the statistical expert on the panel discovered, that Chris was considering a control group. Nor could he be induced to specify sample numbers and general dismay was created by his commenting that he might possibly study only one subject. Invited to discuss his proposed methodology, he talked of geometrical models and cited names which no one there had heard of . Utterly baffled, the panel chairman asked him to wait outside while the board discussed his proposal among themselves.

When the door closed on Chris, those present gave voice to their confusion. How was this strange fish to be regarded? Were we dealing with someone who was reprehensibly vague and muddled or with a genuinely original mind? Did the incomprehensibility of Chris's project derive from the board's own intellectual limits or from the project's lack of conceptual coherence? Happily for the world of research, the panel decided to give him the benefit of the doubt. But bets were hedged in the contract he was offered. He was advised that he might register for an MPhil which he could later submit for upgrading. This registration was, however, conditional upon his attending two taught courses: on methodology and on the special needs of the deaf. As to supervision, I was nominated for several reasons. In so far as anyone understood the methodology Chris had described, I seemed to come closest. I was also the most 'far out' as a researcher among the panel, and if one thing was agreed about Chris, it was that he was far out. Finally, though I had certainly not grasped the exact nature of his proposal, I sensed real creativity in his approach and felt personal resonance with many of the things he said.

The sense of puzzlement and lack of comprehension with which Chris was met at that initial stage has persisted in many of the contexts with which his research has involved him. His conference papers typically leave his audience at something of a loss. When Chris attends meetings of our own research group, his sensitivity, his gentleness, his caring approach are clearly recognised. But his rare contributions to the discussion are often received with silence; no one is quite sure just what he means. Most seriously of all, the demands on understanding which his work entails have nearly led to his work not being considered either for upgrading or for its final examination. My efforts to find someone who was willing to undertake the upgrading task were ultimately successful only after five possible examiners had turned it down. In psychology, philosophy and mathematics, those approached sent back the work with the comment that its scope was too broad, its concerns too abstract, its language too fearsomely difficult.

Yet, undoubtedly, the research in which Chris is engaged is highly creative. Remote and abstruse it may sound; yet its concerns are profoundly human. And Chris himself has shown in his own therapeutic work how these ideas relate to the fundamental existential problems of living. Their conceptual scope, however, offers an enlargement of meaning across an unusually wide sphere of experience and allows exciting connections to be made between traditionally disparate ideas. In supervising this work, I feel a sense of rare privilege. However difficult it is to grasp what Chris is saying, it remains an honour to be in on the creation of genuinely original meaning.

☐ GRACE

PhD research is always the story of personal movement, and in this group Grace has possibly moved the furthest. This has been true of her at several levels. From her position as an external student outside the group of fellow students, she has gradually become something of a pivot in group meetings. The progression of her research project has been no less dramatic. Originally grounded in the most traditional of research moulds, it has been totally reworked to become located in her personal and living concerns. For Grace, who comes from Hong Kong, is a gambler; and it is gambling which is the topic of her research.

When I first met Grace, it was clear that she was struggling unsupported in a context of complete academic isolation. The situation of external students is inevitably very difficult. There is no supervisor as such, merely an adviser, who may be consulted no more than three times a year. There is no attachment to a department or access to formal or informal academic occasions. In effect, the student must work entirely alone. Hardworking, conscientious and accommodating as she is, Grace had accepted this situation for herself by the time I met her. She felt that she should be able to cope with her own work, within the rules of this type of studentship. It was a long time before she accepted my suggestion that she cease to treat me as an adviser and make instead the same demands on me as any research student makes on their supervisor. She was also hesitant to join the group of research students, feeling that this was something she was not really entitled to do. But once she overcame her reluctance, Grace began to make very active use of supervisory and group support.

Of all the members of the research group, Grace has been the most open, the most personal. The courage with which she has revealed her own vulnerabilities, her needs, her doubts, has often enabled other group members to take similar risks. Her painful disclosures have acted as an emotional catalyst; the problems and difficult feelings she talks about are typically experienced also by others. This has meant that aspects of the research process which tend, all too often, to be hidden as shameful secrets, have been, thanks to Grace, openly shared and explored jointly. Grace's engagement in the group has also helped to shape her own standpoint. She draws directly on the advice and experience of others. And the obvious fascination of fellow students with her knowledge of gambling has confirmed her developing resolve to 'own' her research topic.

If Grace has been the most willing of all the students to acknowledge the problems of PhD research, she also faces unusually heavy pressures as a researcher. Living more than 100 miles from London, she needs, for every tutorial group meeting — at which she is a scrupulously regular attender — to embark on a three-hour journey each way. With a young family and a full-time job in clinical psychology, she is hard put to find spare time for her project. She has to conquer practical difficulties in writing up her research, as English is not her first language. Inevitably, Grace has periods of total despair. Yet from these she always surfaces, draws a deep breath and bravely picks up the pieces, to begin again.

☐ IAN

At first sight the 'straightest' member of the group, Ian is in fact full of surprises. His physical appearance, when I first met him, seemed quite in accord with his job as a civil servant teaching soldiers. Yet this was a man who loved birds and who had built ponds, chosen particular trees and shrubs, and left parts of his garden uncultivated, to attract wildlife. For all that his intellectual background was in Maths and Physics, he was well up in reading the latest 'soft' psychology. When at our first encounter we talked about my possible supervision of his project, his obvious fascination with personal construct psychology made a bond between us.

However, Ian is by no means sold on a thorough-going constructivism in social science. He is perfectly willing to live with his own ambivalence and doubt. Using open-ended methods in his own research, he wonders constantly whether they can offer really firm ground. Aware of the importance of subjectivity, he is still pulled back by his own doubts: is this science? He sees himself as a Jungian extrovert, more interested in things than in people; yet his project calls for an immersion in the painful experience of psychic wounds. Ian has his own way of managing these inner contradictions: he relates them to questions of typology. This allows him to view contrasting approaches as alternative constructions and to see his own uncertainties as the fluctuating movement between analytical science and human particularity.

The history of Ian's research project has itself been the story of just this kind of movement. In keeping with his intellectual adventurousness, he has radically reshaped the direction and the character of his research. This started as the documenting by standardised enquiry methods of personality change in adolescence. The actual project, now nearly complete, entails different subjects, different methods, different kinds of analysis. Ian's focus is no longer on adolescents but on the inarticulate and catastrophic world of the newly brain-injured. Of necessity, standardised rating forms and inventories have been abandoned in favour of ad hoc, difficult, inventive kinds of conversation. Equally inevitably, statistical analysis has given way to the tracing of personal meaning.

In the context of group meetings, Ian struggles with another kind of ambivalence. Temperamentally uncomfortable with the occasional silences which grow out of the preparedness to think together, he is continually tempted to throw in a flippant remark. Yet he is well aware of the necessary tensions of group processes and in his own teaching, to managers, he emphasises the importance of taking time in arriving at decisions. A conscientious and friendly attender, he remains a somewhat unpredictable participant.

☐ JOCELYN

Into my office one October afternoon walked a woman of remarkable physical presence. In one hand she carried a smart briefcase, in the other a carry-cot with a tiny baby. This was Jocelyn, whose personal bearing seems to illustrate the meaning of Black pride. In fact this occasion was one of considerable stress on her side. Happy with her first child, she was nevertheless facing life as a single parent. She had given birth prematurely, following the shock of her car being stolen. As later transpired, Jocelyn also carried serious doubts as to her interview with me, most seriously as to whether her own research intentions would be respected. Nothing of all this, however, was apparent in her supremely confident manner.

If, in applying to register for a PhD at the Institute, Jocelyn was apprehensive about the likely fate of her research proposal, her recent experience gave her good reason. Trained as a clinical psychologist, she had become deeply interested in developmental issues around racial identity and their implications for young Black children. She hoped to explore these issues further by assessing the impact of positive self-reference material on children in Black supplementary schools. Her interest had been supported and encouraged on a visit to the US, where she found her concerns affirmed by a number of academics who understood and shared them. Back in the UK, however, it was a different story. Those she approached as potential supervisors expressed reluctance to take on the kind of project she had in mind. Either she was advised to drop her anti-racist stance and base her work in the 'neutral' orientation of traditional developmental psychology, or else she found her concern with race subsumed and translated into issues of gender, within a feminist perspective. The fact that she was pregnant proved a further obstacle: 'Wait and see, my dear, you may not be interested in all this once your baby is born.'

So much discouragement, which would have deterred many a would-be research student, made no dent in the resolve of Jocelyn, who is nothing if not determined. She had, it emerged when we first met, already made day-care arrangements for her daughter and had set up space and time within the limits of her full-time job to carry out her field work. The person I met that afternoon was visibly dynamic and resourceful, with a project to which she was clearly committed and to which she brought special insight and expertise. It was not until many months later that Jocelyn told me of her expectations at the time: of her battle-weary apprehension that yet another white woman would make a feminist take-over, of her grim determination that come what may she would stick to her guns and maintain her primary focus on race.

In that early interview, Jocelyn felt that her voice was heard and realised that she would be able to negotiate her own research undertaking rather than being subjected to authoritarian directives. But as a Black woman she remained, throughout the ultimately successful progress of her work, keenly alive to the whiteness of her academic context and its ever-present possibilities for disregarding, even violating, her personal standpoint. To a white supervisor such as myself, these possibilities were not always obvious,. Qualitative methods, for example, may raise issues to do with personal disclosure: issues which need to be carefully weighed by a Black researcher in a white racist society. Through working with Jocelyn, I came to a new understanding of some aspects of the significance of race in human science research.

☐ LESLEY

Practical, earthy, sensuous as she is, Lesley seems an unlikely Doctor of Philosophy. Can this person, who nurtures hedgehogs and ailing plants, savours exotic herbs and spices, eagerly explores new landscapes and relationships alike — can this person also have achieved a PhD? Lesley carries her doctorate with the same lightness and humour as she bears her own life heritage. It is a heritage which would have crushed many women. Yet throughout the strains and pressures of impoverished single motherhood, with three young children to support, she has always kept her hope, her zest, her youthfulness. Lesley refuses to accept conventional restraints on what she does or the closing off of possibilities that many women in their fifties would bow to. For her, life remains excitingly open.

Lesley's progression to the achievement of a PhD has been anything but easy and straightforward. The concerns of her own parents focused primarily on feeding their five children and, like the families around them, they were especially indifferent to the education of their daughters. She did not even take the 11 plus, left her Secondary Modern school at fifteen, and worked for twenty-seven shillings a week in a local department store. Married at eighteen to a Roman Catholic, she was by twenty already the mother of two. Not until her mid-thirties did she begin the long climb to qualify for university, labouring through a succession of O and A levels while simultaneously working and caring for her family. This achievement was personally costly. Though she did most of her studying after the children had gone to bed or before they woke up, both they and she felt that this was time stolen from mothering time. For all her sense that these efforts were a preparation for their shared future, Lesley could not escape feelings of guilt.

Eventually Lesley graduated and, thanks to a grant for mature learners, went on to do a Masters degree. She then took a research post in Birmingham as part of a team funded by the Department of Health and Social Security, which was to consider preparation for parenthood in secondary schools. Intensely interested as she was in this topic, Lesley's experience of funded research was not without bitterness. The team's findings and conclusions, which took account of the importance of class and gender, were entirely bypassed in a report which uncritically recommended making the existing curriculum compulsory. She decided that if she was to explore questions that were genuinely her own in her own way, without pressures from others in positions of power over research, she would need to take on an independent post-graduate project. It was at this point that Lesley registered for a PhD.

Lesley's PhD research on preparation for parenthood as an ideological discourse is essentially grounded within her own life experience. Issues about the preparing of young people for their probable future roles as parents are not for her merely academic questions. There are personal underpinnings in the fact that it is girls, and working-class girls at that, at whom this curriculum is really aimed, and in the observation that, as a discourse, preparation for parenthood helps to legitimate policies which ensure the continuation of an impoverished sector of society. Her research project has represented a personal quest to understand her own life history — a history which was so nearly a living out of the socio-economic destiny of working class women.

☐ MAGGIE

When I first met Maggie, nine years ago, she was a student training as a professional educational psychologist — a training to which I made some contribution. Though I did not know it at the time, this was one step on a long journey from school failure to the highest levels of education, in pursuit of an intellectual enquiry which is very much her own. For all that both her parents held first class honours degrees, Maggie herself found school tough, and failed the 11 plus. However, she persisted with her school studies and was subsequently able to take a teacher training. It was not until her early thirties that she felt the need to undertake degree work. This decision resulted in four years' hard slog, four nights a week at Birkbeck College, from where she graduated with a degree in psychology. She then moved into training as an educational psychologist and has worked in this field for the last eight years. The distinction with which she completed her training gave her the confidence to register for a higher research degree. It is as supervisor of her research project that I know her.

Throughout this long and difficult educational progression, what has carried Maggie along has been a kind of intellectual stubbornness, an obstinate refusal to accept the conventional wisdom about the nature of learning. One aspect of this has to do with her determination to disprove the ascriptions to which she herself was subject as a school pupil — to demonstrate to herself that she has a brain and she can use it. But more specifically, she is fired by a passionate and long-standing anger at the disservice which orthodox psychology has done to parents, teachers and children, in the account it offers of learning to read. Maggie believes that this account utterly fails to deliver anything which makes sense to teachers who have the daily responsibility of teaching young children. For anxious parents whose children are finding learning to read difficult, the almost magical solutions implied by experimental psychology can only encourage vain hopes. And for young beginning readers struggling to grapple with the mystery of print, the failure to recognise their social, emotional and cultural context means ignoring the very factors which are critical to success or failure.

To challenge academic orthodoxy in this field requires considerable courage. Of all areas of psychology, its account of the reading process is perhaps the most daunting. Yet Maggie is making her own way through the abstruse theoretical literature, the often mystifying language, the highly complex experimental analyses. Unintimidated by it all, she is thoughtfully, carefully, patiently working towards a redescription of the reading process in terms of a coherent whole. This means testing conceptual accounts of learning to read within the crucible of her own involvement as a participant observer working with young beginning readers. Determinedly avoiding easy generalisations, she insists on incorporating awkward facts which may not fit a simple, intellectually elegant account. Resolved to do justice to the ideas of others, she nevertheless maintains her own course, not aligning herself with any existing camp.

All this calls for a high level of intellectual autonomy: something which is evident not only in Maggie's pursuit of her project but also in the way she takes personal charge and personal responsibility for the place this project is to have in her life. To an unusual degree, she has worked out the practicalities of part-time research: the money, the organisation of materials, the time and space which are involved in fitting a project into a busy family life which also involves a shared enthusiasm for sailing. Careful and caring, with a sometimes painful integrity, Maggie conveys a sense of strong commitment to the research she has undertaken.

☐ QADIR

To meet Qadir is to see at once why he has been outstandingly successful in his work as a Community Relations Officer and Race Relations Adviser. Urbane, genial, courteous, he conveys a sense of professional responsibility confidently carried, a personal poise seemingly unthreatened by the conflicts and tensions endemic in the field of multicultural relations. He is that rare person: an immigrant who has 'made it' but who continues to dedicate himself to the vast majority of Black people at the sharp end of a racist society.

In the context of the PhD selection board where I first encountered him, it was Qadir's wide experience of multicultural and anti-racist work, together with his obvious personal commitment, which impressed every board member. Taken together with his academic credentials, this experience seemed to offer great potential; he was a candidate about whom we were all agreed. Yet paradoxically the duality of Qadir's involvement in his research sphere has proved problematic.

Qadir's life has for many years been committed to the articulation of Black oppression and the development of life chances for those involved. His PhD topic is the political situation of Black teenagers. This concern is equally close to his heart as Head of a Race Relations Unit in a London borough. And, in his own corner, Qadir has made a real impact on the situation. Working with community grassroots organisations and with the local authority, in committee work, publications and informal contacts, he has succeeded in raising public consciousness and in beginning to change both attitudes and policies. In the course of this work, Qadir has also acquired something of a national profile.

It is, though, the very success of Qadir's professional work which in some sense undermines his position as a PhD researcher. His wide experience of effective intervention as promoting social change puts a question mark over the usefulness of an academic research project. Given the urgency of achieving justice for ethnic and cultural minorities, should not all his energies be devoted to the direct and practical tasks entailed by his job? There are, in any case, currently intense pressures on the field of race relations work. Many boroughs have abolished their Race Relations Units; and among those that remain, Black chief officers are characteristically expected to perform at a higher level and to achieve more than their white peers. Simply to maintain the existence of his post, Qadir works every evening and at weekends; his job entails an endless treadmill of report-writing every six weeks. It is perhaps hardly surprising that he has never yet found it possible to set aside the resources of time and energy for a sustained onslaught on the research. Despite the many years we have worked together (for Qadir is the longest-registered member of the group), the work remains incomplete. Though the data-gathering is finished, the writing up is not begun.

There is a further, equally positive reason why Qadir has not been able to complete his PhD. As with many other mature students, he is committed to his family. But in Qadir's case, his family life is yet another project in the cause of Black championship. His pride in having a young writer-daughter, his deep personal investment in the mixed-race daughter he has just adopted — these do not stand apart from his professional and research commitment but are essentially a part of it. Qadir is perhaps an unusually integrated man, but such integration may prove to have its cost, in terms of a never-to-be-completed PhD.

☐ SHEILA

Quick in her intuitive perceptions, Sheila astonished her fellow students when, a few years ago, she attended a group meeting for the first time. At my suggestion, the students were working through an exercise designed to explore questions of time. The task entailed placing oneself and fellow group members on an imaginary line which went from the start to the completion of the project. Though Sheila had met the others only half an hour before and had talked only of the most general matters, her guesses as to how they were experiencing the progression of their projects were extraordinarily accurate.

In her own research work, Sheila's perceptiveness is equally striking. The project gives vivid voice to young people who tend to feel isolated from the formal processes of learning, and for whom much of official school business seems irrelevant to their way of life. That Sheila can act as spokesperson for such views is itself remarkable for someone who has been a teacher for nearly two decades. In coming to know her, however, I soon became aware that her stance was never, in the conventional sense, a teacherly one.

Like many girls who drift into teaching, Sheila had no clear career ambitions and simply opted for a profession that was generally popular among young women. Since sport was the subject she had most enjoyed at school, she trained as a teacher of Physical Education. She taught in Scotland for a number of years before joining the Inner London Education Authority. At that period teaching was becoming an all graduate profession and Sheila duly registered for a part-time BEd degree which she obtained at honours level somewhat to her own surprise. She decided to take an MSc in Health Education, a sphere in which she was becoming involved through pastoral work at school. Following this further qualification, Sheila returned to a school post which was mainly concerned with Careers Education and Guidance. It was here, above all, that she became acutely aware of the disaffection of many young people with their school lives. When an opportunity arose to undertake a research project into pupils' perceptions of stress in school, she took the post; and it is this project which constitutes her PhD.

If Sheila is able to articulate the mismatch between school life and the concerns of school pupils, this certainly has to do with her own sense of herself. Despite her impressive string of academic qualifications, she still lacks confidence in her own intellectual ability: her pupil status as not clever, not academic, not university material is perhaps an indelible part of her own self-image. But though this creates discomfort in her role as a PhD student, it immeasurably strengthens the quality of her material. The voices to be heard most clearly in her research are not those of confident, successful pupils, but the voices of unacademic young people seldom listened to in school: voices struggling to express inarticulate feelings of anxiety, frustration, rage.

Sheila's own situation as a research student differs in two important ways from that of other group members. She is not registered in London, where she lives, but in Edinburgh and her project is full-time and funded (though ungenerously). Both these facts make a significant impact on her experience as a researcher. Her situation entails a virtual deprivation of adequate official supervision. Geographical distance is complicated by staff inexperience and by the dislocations of institutional mergers and reorganisation. Sheila's status as a full-time, funded student, for all its apparent advantages, also carries its own problems. A sense of accountability to others, together with the lack of a legitimate escape into paid employment, can further intensify already heavy subjective pressures.When I first met her, Sheila was very much at the sharp end of a difficult situation. I offered to take her on informally as a supervisee and a member of the student group. Characteristically, Sheila was hesitant to take up the offer, feeling that she was not entitled to so much support. Eventually she took me at my word. With her quiet courage, her humour, her delicacy of feeling, she has proved to be a most rewarding person with whom to work.

□ SUSAN

Susan is in academic terms undoubtedly the most experienced and the most confident of the group. Her expertise has been critically important to more than one fellow-student. 'Since Susan has lent me Lincoln and Cuba, I've felt so excited/been so much more confident/I really begin to see the way forward.' Her accomplishments are the fruits of an unusually interesting and adventurous intellectual journey.

It was when Susan was on her way to Harvard to do a PhD that the illness of a family member brought her to the UK, where she remained. In this context she met the very barriers in higher education which were to become the concern of her own project: the rich experience which she had acquired in the US counted for nothing when it came to the question of university access. Susan had worked with both difficult and gifted teenagers, using creative arts therapeutic approaches. Out of this work, she had come to collaborate with the eminent psychologist Paul Torrance and later to lead a development programme within a consortium of colleges and universities in New Orleans. This programme for undergraduates who would be working with young people was pioneering in its emphasis on learning concerns and its use of field placements and self and peer assessment methods.

The American context in which this work was done not only acted to block Susan's entry to PhD registration, it also restricted the kinds of professional work she was able to undertake in Britain. Nevertheless, she managed with enterprise and resourcefulness to find openings within the restrictions of her work permit, which allowed her to develop her interests in adult learning in the fields of social work, education and healthcare, eventually establishing a national trainer training programme for people working in continuing professional development.

Throughout these years, Susan never abandoned her resolve to pursue her own higher education and it was in the university setting that I met her. After I had given a lecture to a common course for students taking various teaching diplomas, a number of people came to speak to me. One of them stood out as quite unusual among the teachers of special needs who constituted the regular course participants: an extremely pleasant and forthcoming woman whose obvious sophistication in the academic sphere came as a surprise.

It at once became clear that Susan felt herself to be misplaced. She was there to jump a series of hurdles. Since her American qualifications were not in her field of choice for postgraduate study, she had to start almost from scratch if she wanted to register for a PhD. Provided she took the diploma course satisfactorily, she might then move on to the Masters, following which she would be eligible for a research degree. In the event, this lengthy sequence was cut short and Susan was even appointed to an academic post within the university. But during this first encounter, I sensed the urgency of her concern and soon became aware that in her academic isolation my interest and support were a kind of lifeline. I was impressed by her commitment, her determination to pursue a personal quest which the academic authorities were making maximally hard to achieve. When she approached me later as a possible supervisor, her personal dedication was for me the decisive factor. And in the finally triumphant progression of her PhD work, with all its inevitable ups and downs, the depth of Susan's own investment has never been in doubt. Not only has she desired the doctorate as a supreme personal achievement, it has also offered her the opportunity of exploring, through the eyes of mature learners — particularly women learners — her own experiences as a learner within and outside institutions of higher education.

Chapter Four

The PhD Undertaking

'The business of tackling a PhD', writes Sheila,

> was very different from anything I had done previously. For example, no prior academic undertaking allowed me such scope and I found the freedom both frightening and challenging. The other, taught, courses which I had followed offered prescribed reading lists, lectures on specific topics followed by an examination dealing with the work covered during the course. Such a format (with which I was accustomed since my schooldays) organised within strictly defined parameters, offered a certain security. In contrast, the PhD thesis (especially at the beginning) was, for me, vast and amorphous.

PhD and MPhil differ crucially from every other kind of academic degree, in being awarded for the student's own original work. Unlike a certificate, a diploma, a Bachelors or Masters degree, a doctorate does not merely entail the consideration of already existing work within a pre-arranged structure but demands the creation of a personal project. To undertake a PhD is therefore to define oneself as having a contribution to make to understanding in the area concerned. As Ann remarks, 'The essential difference with this degree is that there is not the external structure imposed by the nature of a taught course. I chose the MPhil route — I felt I had a contribution to make to knowledge.'

As will be evident from the account of the topics involved in this group's projects, all the students here feel a personal investment in their own research sphere, and a need to define and pursue their own enquiry within it. In this sense, each believes that they have a unique contribution to offer. This is most clearly spelt out by Lesley:

> My registration for post-graduate research marked the point when it
> seemed essential to look at questions which were mine, in my own
> way, without pressure from those who felt greater ownership of the
> research and its outcomes. I wanted the commitment to a study that
> registration would give me; I wanted the political freedom to investi-
> gate my own concerns, design my own study and develop appropriate
> methodology.

There are several strands in Lesley's educational experience which, as she
describes, led her to this point. One such strand was the development, during
her Masters course, of a critical attitude towards her academic mentors. One
day she made a presentation to a seminar, based on the assumption that
working class culture represents a valid culture, rather than merely a state
of deprivation. The presentation was:

> welcomed by other students but was not accepted by the professor,
> who maintained an angry silence throughout ... This was perhaps the
> first time I had been disappointed in someone I had until then regarded
> as 'a teacher': someone who had a store of useful knowledge, and
> someone whose duty was to impart as much of it as possible to me.
> Mulling and puzzling over his reaction included a vestigial thought
> that perhaps this was protection of privilege made manifest.

Another strand was the transformation, during the course of carrying it out,
of her Masters dissertation. Lesley had initially expected this mini-thesis to
be 'a kind of sampler, such as those letters produced by embroiderers,
demonstrating their expertise. My dissertation started like that, designed to
demonstrate my handling of literature, research design, research techniques,
statistics, analysis and report writing.' As she began to engage with the issues
she had chosen to examine, this model did, of course, prove quite inadequate.
Lesley came to see her task as evolving her own meanings.

Because it entails the creation of an original project, the PhD undertaking
calls for a very high level of intellectual autonomy and personal responsibility. To few students are these implications fully evident when they begin
their work. Nor, once launched on their projects, is it always possible to
avoid slipping back into more familiar, safer learning modes. Sheila, conscious of the threats as well as the exhilaration in the openness of this
undertaking, illustrates this experience.

> To have to set my own boundaries and define my own research was
> extremely daunting and there were many times when I longed for the
> strictures of a taught course and for someone to tell me what to do.
> There have been many occasions when I have felt as if I was in a maze
> and totally lost. However, unlike a maze it was not a case of looking
> for some well-defined, if perhaps difficult to locate route out. Having

made my own path in, it was up to me to make my own path out again ... I see the undertaking of a PhD as a pioneering one.

Sheila goes on to describe how difficult it is to find one's own path in the maze, to work autonomously, without external direction:

I frequently feel so confused that I experience difficulty in formulating questions to ask concerning the next step in my research. When I do succeed, it frequently appears that the answer is, 'It depends.' It depends on what I want. So often I do not know what I want and I long for someone to tell me, or give me some sort of clue. Although part of me appreciates that the research is mine and I have the freedom to choose what I find out and how I go about this, another part of me cannot, or will not, accept this freedom. I continue to behave as if the answer lies 'out there' somewhere and if only I can find the solution (rather like a koan puzzle) all will be revealed and I can move forward. Of course, research is not like that.

Maggie's account touches a similar theme:

I am still haunted by the idea that there is a particular book or article that would be the golden answer to all my difficulties, and I still frequently leaf great hunks of text when I feel I have nothing to say of any value ... My confidence dips and it is hard for anyone to help me. This is surely the nub of doing research; in a way, no one can help in terms of telling me what to do. This is the antithesis of the whole of the rest of our educational system. There isn't something laid down already for me to learn. I am on my own trying to do a very tiny bit of something which I think is original.

For everyone who undertakes to do a PhD, the experience is unprecedented; no one has ever been just there before. What the project means becomes known only through doing it. For Sheila, nearing the end of her work, her enquiry is only now beginning to take a clear shape:

I have completed the fieldwork for my research and have written the first three chapters of my thesis. However, it is only as I have completed each of the many steps necessary to bring me to this stage that I have been able to stand back and appreciate exactly what I have done. Whilst engaged in the process I feel rather like a person groping about in the dark, in a maze. It is only on emerging into the daylight that I am aware of a feeling 'So that's what it was all about'. I rather suspect that only when I have successfully completed my PhD will I really feel equipped to tackle it.

Another reason why the PhD undertaking can become defined only through actually doing it, is that what may have started as an apparently simple question is apt, through research, to be transformed — becoming perhaps infinitely more complicated. This is an aspect with which Ian has been concerned:

> One model of the PhD process shows how uncertainty reduces with time. The model is presented as a diagram. The uncertainty is shown as a triangle which is at its widest at the start of the study and reduces linearly and uniformly to zero when the study is completed. At the stage I am at — writing up — the diagram shows that the uncertainty is nearly zero. Subjectively for me, this is far from the case ... It has often been remarked that each answer that you find in research poses many questions. This knowledge expands geometrically. In this case the model should not only be reversed but the triangle should be turned into a musical horn shape ... being confused at a higher level. That is, what appeared to be simple and straightforward turns out to be anything but. This is true, I think, of any non-trivial issue one takes on in life, particularly one with practical implications for human beings. If the research process was so simple, suggesting that the problem was simple, was there really much point in investigating it? ... Most real problems are complex, soft, fuzzy, messy, vicious and wicked (to use some technical terms which have been applied to describe them). My experience of research leads me to see it as the reverse of the triangle ... I think it was Robert Owen who said 'All things I thought I knew, but now confess, the more I know, I know I know the less'. That's certainly the feeling I've got through this process.

At the beginning of PhD research, it is perhaps impossible to foresee what this unique undertaking will entail, what personal demands it will make, or how it will feel. To Grace, the project turned out to be very different from what she had anticipated:

> When I first registered for the external PhD degree it felt like a good idea. There was absolutely no understanding of how much time and what sort of commitment I would have to set myself. The part-time registration for five years seemed a long way away and surely I must be able to finish that before the set time. Such naivety almost undermined the work of research which I was treating as a piece of homework, along traditional experimental lines. The simplistic approach to such commitment also reflected my lack of self discipline and time set aside for the continuation of such work ... I felt that after the fieldwork everything would be straightforward but alas, I was so wrong in making these assumptions.

As she describes, Grace has suffered severe problems and setbacks in the course of her PhD work:

> During my eight years of pursual to my writing up of the research, I was astonished how much stress I have had to cope with apart from

the PhD worries. Physically I had three operations like lump in the breast, hernia, and suspected transient ischaemic accidents, which could be explained in terms of stresses caused due to the present job demands, children growing up and a demanding husband. All these had to be coped with over and above my internal worries of self-efficacy, determination in completing my PhD.

Inevitably, these difficulties have brought Grace times of emotional turmoil:

There were constant mixed up emotional states throughout these years. The moods grew from stability to elation when I felt that I discovered something new, to total despair when I felt lost. The anger was often projected to my immediate family members and I felt that they could help me in other minor chores so as to let me carry on with my aspiration when that happened. Very often when I needed the time I could not have it due to others' demands. I have exploded when I had enough of the stress. My husband who was unwilling or unable to help because it was not his priority. The guilt that people managed to stir in me was incredible: a wife, a mother, a full-time clinician, why would I need to continue my PhD?

If Grace's situation as a PhD student is particularly fraught with difficulty, this does not mean that others, whose personal circumstances are somewhat easier, can escape such experiences as she describes. A universal theme among these students is that of intellectual and emotional vicissitude. As Ann remarks, 'There is the uncertainty about the value of the work I have done — despondency mostly seems to be the essence of research and these feelings are shared by each one of us about our own work.' For Maggie, there are spasmodic inner doubts which throw a spanner in the works of her ongoing research:

The main block which stops me from progressing with my study is the frequent loss of confidence which hits me whenever I least expect it. These losses can debilitate me for a long period (almost a year at one point) or just for an evening. I am learning how to cope with my wimpishness with the help of my supervisor, husband and boss, and through sharing with other research students. The shared understanding and support enables me to chug and sputter along. I am coming to realise that this sort of progress is OK and I may eventually finish the wretched thing.

PhD projects have long histories. For Chris, personal vicissitude has taken the form of varying closeness, or distance from, the project he has been conducting:

By having my research project as a focus over time, I have been able to use it to address some questions and issues which I feel are important. Looking back now from this present time-frame, it is difficult to say to what extent at different times I have been consciously aware of making use of the project as such a focus. It seems that upon certain levels of awareness I have used this focus for wider development from its early days but, certainly, over the years this has become more intentionally conscious. During this time the explicit and stated content and themes have changed more than once. From the outside, such changes may have appeared erratic but from the inside I felt, and feel, that there has been a consistency ...

During my time of having the research project 'in mind', it has sometimes been very much to the fore and at others more in the background. I have orbited around this changing focus, sometimes closely and at other times at a great distance. It seems to me there is always the risk, in orbiting at a great distance, that we may travel so far away from the 'gravity' of the attracting focus of our project, we may, for all kinds of reasons, abandon or drift away forever from our research project ... If we 'orbit at a great distance' and do not lose the 'pull' of our project, we may bring back to it a much wider perspective.

Original research is a process with intrinsic ups and downs; and Lesley expresses a common theme, for the members of this group in referring to her own experiential lability:

In addition to lucky moments and great fulfilment associated with being in charge of an investigation into what felt like a mystery of social importance, my experience of research has included long dragging periods, filled with feelings of impotence, exasperation and lack of direction. Progress over the years was slow and uneven; employment commitments were such that I had no time to work on my research for months on end and, when I did find time, I often wasted it in blind alleys.

PhD study can, for many students, demand difficult kinds of integration. This is particularly likely to be the case where those involved are mature people, who must somehow achieve a marriage between their own lived experience as professional adults and the formal structures and language modes of the academic world. In this group, it is perhaps Ann who feels this dilemma most acutely. Here, she gives voice to the conflict she experiences between the role of professional teacher — a role she inhabits and respects — and the role of academic — a role she deeply mistrusts, yet, as a doctoral student must take on.

The position of a professional may be seen as being in opposition to that of an academic. The professional is also the practical and it must be recognised that the professional is operating with the theoretical basis and bringing about the theoretical, academic evolution. The professional is making the knowledge, monitoring, refining and re-peating, again and again. The creation is really by the professional — the academic is the one who takes, measures, then pronounces — or theorises — not the one who shapes — the shaping is done by the person who is the practitioner ... Without the teaching it could be a very strong possibility that very little advances are made for humanity and for academics. To teach, one has to be the facilitator, enabler, informer — unless this is done no one will 'do' anything in any meaningful way that advances human knowledge ...

The teaching has not occurred because of an academic — the academic it seems to me is retrospective — examining what has gone — the academic does not inform the classroom; the classroom informs the academic — the academic is informed by the practices of humanity. An academic cannot exist in a vacuum or in isolation. The dictionary definition of academic reads: 'of purely theoretical or speculative interest; excessively concerned with intellectual matters and lacking experience of practical affairs'. My case is that the theoretical or speculative interest is not possible without the practice.

Continuing to argue with herself, Ann angrily counters what she sees as the disrespect accorded to professional people such as herself:

I would challenge the notion of the professional being a 'nobody' — could it be that this notion is only in the academic world? do practi-tioners accept they are nobodies? could it be that the elevated position of the academic is really only cared about and for, by the academic themselves? aren't the rest of us only really impressed by those who invent, who discover new knowledge?

Anchoring the exaggerated respect for academics, Ann concludes, is 'the power of print' and it is through this mode that she is able to find common ground between her two worlds, seeing the written word as equally import-ant to both.

It is the power of print that is currently above all else — if information is 'in print' it has an enormous, impossible power; print carries great weight. My own experience of an article published in 1984 on anti-racist teaching is evidence of this — it still gets an occasional mention by people I know — the TES at the time referred to the article ... If the same words are merely verbal or unpublished, they carry very little weight. It is a strange position — and my conclusion really is that for professionals and lay people it is the written word that is powerful, in academia it is the philosophical printed word that is powerful — and I don't think that this distinction diminishes the value of either.

In a different way, Qadir also experiences uncomfortable disjunctions between the role of a PhD student and his role as a professional worker in the field of race relations. For Qadir, the problem centres on writing. The demands of a PhD thesis are quite unlike the demands of the kind of professional report he regularly undertakes in his daily work.

> I have been involved in professional research projects and have published a lot, and have never felt uncomfortable — my audience is very wide-ranging — some people somewhere have definitely benefited as individuals or groups — policy makers, professionals, community groups. I am very much used to producing for policy development and seeing the results over the years. But I have not mastered skills, confidence, to satisfy academia. It is very restrictive compared with the above situation, where the range of readership is very wide. The problem, peculiar to my situation, is that of my two roles: policy development and academic work. I have to unlearn certain aspects of each aspect of my life, to satisfy both. I cannot use academic terminology and theory per se in policy/community development work, and vice versa.

Both Ann and Qadir bring to academic study an ambivalence which is rooted in their experience as responsible professionals. For Chris, there have been doubts of another kind. As he describes, to pursue a higher degree has seemed at times to be merely a self-indulgence, an empty exercise:

> There was a time I seriously questioned continuing with a PhD, because I considered it to be an over-privileged position and project. Perhaps it was better to get on with trying to change at least some aspects of 'the world' in other ways. Indeed, I have known others who decided — quite validly for them — that they would give up their post-graduate project. This was one of the difficult times. I mentioned this to the person supervising my project — that it was perhaps a sheer indulgence, reserved mostly for middle and upper class people or those who had entered into these contexts; an indirect collusion with 'establishment' values. Having at times been upon the negative underside — the receiving end — of such establishment structures, this was not only an armchair ideological position but one I felt. She asked me whether this meant that I considered all her students' works as well as her own to be conformist. I did not, for such works and others had given me encouragement, inspiration, and resonated for me. This was a seed. I eventually came to the conclusion that such a decision did not have to be an 'either/or' but that it could be an 'and', and so continued. There appeared to be many research projects which were plugged into 'mainstream psychology' and were, unintentionally, further sedimenting refined structures. So it seemed worthwhile to persist in developing alternative structures which might contribute to alternative ways of

making sense of human experiencing; and so to some limited extent possibly adds a 'counterweight' to these.

From these accounts it is very clear that PhD study is no easy option. Intrinsic to such work is a lack of outer structures and direction; a feature which, while it allows necessary autonomy, can also leave the student floundering. The way forward may seem to become not clearer but more obscure as time goes on; and people may accumulate a sense of wasted time, wasted work, through the blind alleys, the wrong turnings they have travelled. For no one is there ever enough time. Research needs large spaces; yet these remain merely a luxurious fantasy amongst the day-to-day pressures of busy adult lives. Nor is it only outer obstacles which students face. If there are moments of excitement, of joy, of insight, there are also many moments of anxiety, doubt and despair: as Ann remarks, despondency is the name of the game. In the absence of a set curriculum, an explicit criterion, agreed kinds of competence, students are, to a terrifying extent, on their own. This situation has built-in doubts and uncertainties for those involved as to the value of their enterprise. Given all this, it seems hardly surprising that the students writing here describe the research process as a struggle — or even, as Grace puts it, as an 'albatross'. What is perhaps much more surprising is that, despite all the difficulties, every one of these students remains committed.

Facing the problems of being a PhD student, how do people cope? Different individuals do, of course, evolve different strategies. One student who has written of her struggle not to abandon the whole enterprise is Grace.

> There were moments that I wished that I had never contemplated doing a PhD, was it vanity, was it torture? ... Very often I felt that I came to the end of the road ... It was not until I had my peer group and supervisory support and encouragement that I even tried to be more productive and creative in my work. The ownership of my own work began to feel stronger, and I felt more confident in defending myself and my thoughts.

This came about gradually, as Grace found ways of dealing with the difficult moments in her research:

> There have been moments when it was hard to restimulate or motivate myself, particularly in times of failure and despair. This cycle of emotional swings has been a common occurrence. It was important then for me to forget about the research for a while so that I could recuperate. I indulged in relaxing, doing nothing and pursuing my new hobbies like painting, stamp collecting and authentic cooking lessons. The space and time to myself proved to be tremendously useful and I often bounced back. It was the ability to cope with failure which fluctuated from time to time; if the other bits in my life were not as bad, or remotely positive, it helped more in coming to terms with

setbacks in writing up. The standards that I set myself have also got to be realistic. I fluctuated from being perfectionist to nihilistic. These expectations did not necessarily help at all, because they fed into the vicious circle of failures and inadequacies. So I had to remind myself constantly to be aware of my own expectations and of others in order to keep afloat.

Like Grace, Susan has had to fight despair and to resist the temptation to give up, even at a very late stage in her work: 'To my dismay, I learned that even when you are into your second draft, you can still be tempted to give up altogether.' She believes she was rescued by the determination and support of her supervisor, who continued to assert her belief in the power and value of what she was doing, and by her friend and fellow-student, who 'was always there when I needed to rant and rave.'

Maggie, too, wrestles with her doubts as to her own value of what she has undertaken:

I frequently wonder why on earth I want to do the study. How nice it would be not to have it hanging over me, but that's the strange thing about it. I don't have to do it, except to prove to myself that I can.'

Defining the project as something essentially belonging to her has been important for Maggie:

I have slowly come to realise that much of my early motivation for the study was to do with trying to impress my parents. This has given way to something more personal to me rather than my family.

Like Grace, she has discovered how to avoid particularly undermining experiences and to allow herself as much support as possible:

I need to have quite a strong feeling of self-confidence to keep going with the work. I need consciously to seek out experiences that will boost me and avoid those likely to knock me down ... I have not told many people about my work and have avoided writing articles or giving papers. ... So far I have written safe things, details of observations, ideas about methodology, and a start on a literature review.

Gradually she is finding a sense of increasing confidence in the undertaking:

From time to time I have looked at other people's PhDs and draw confidence from a feeling that what I have read is not beyond my capability ... Not long ago a colleague who has a PhD asked me why I was bothering to do it? This was very disturbing coming from her. But somehow in struggling to answer her, I have found new energy and hope to carry on, and the process of explaining my area of interest to her left me feeling quite 'high'.

Maggie is now able, despite inevitable moments of doubt, to describe her study in positive colours:

> I have slowly come to realise that I have a lot of sort of inner confidence in my knowledge and experience in the area of my study. Although I haven't spent much time in writing over the last few years, in some ways I have lived, slept and eaten it for what feels like for ever! ... You see, I know that I know something. I don't know what it is, and I am looking forward to finding out what it is when I finally write about it!

For these PhD students, what keeps them going is the sense of personal creation, the knowledge that the project they are struggling to complete is something which they alone can offer. Lesley, looking back on her own recently completed study, describes the experience as both 'bloody hard work' and 'wonderful': 'It's wonderful to have a question, to be desperate to answer it, and then to work systematically through to the answer.' The process is, however, as she also insists, a risky one. Her own study meant that 'I missed out on so much: on fun and love and rest'. And, as Susan's frankly told experience testifies, research can indeed carry heavy personal costs:

> Little did I know how this enquiry would really challenge and change me. Oh yes, I learned a great deal about other people's stories: about how their life and work experience shaped how they made sense of themselves as learners and learning in higher education. But what I could not have envisaged at the beginning was the extent to which I would learn so much about my own story. And having embarked on this journey, it was immensely difficult to turn back. The pressures that such a major undertaking places upon an already busy life in terms of time and space are considerable. But little did I know about the strain my own growth was to place on my marriage. Little significant learning is without pain or struggle. Those closest to you are inevitably drawn into that struggle. Also, as I came to understand better critical influences upon my own identity and started to work through their consequences, my own voice and strengths as a woman became clearer.

> There were those who delighted in this development and in my growing courage to express who I was, rather than merely to facilitate others. Others did not find it so easy, including my husband. On the surface, he actively supported my progress. But, sensing his gradual withdrawal, I would often express my concern that he was holding back things that could only damage us in the long term. I used to plead with him to be open, and not to let us go under for the sake of 'just a PhD'. He continued to assert that no, everything was fine. He continued to take the greater share of household tasks. But as he said to a

friend, several months after we split up, he realised how much responsibility I had taken previously for the 'real work' of our relationship.
During those last two years of the PhD, I was suddenly not there in the
same way. And instead of allowing us space to work through what we
were both experiencing in terms of our relationship, and to make
informed choices about our future if that were necessary, he chose to
find another woman on whom to lean. Who was just starting on her
career. Whom he could, once again, set upon the first steps of a journey.
By the time I got the PhD, it was far too late. And the damage of so
much unnecessary lying and denial, of so much confusion and guilt,
was immense.'

For all that her PhD cost Susan her marriage, she is, nevertheless, finally
able to affirm its profound personal value:

So was this whole undertaking worthwhile? For a long time, my
successfully completed thesis came to symbolise nothing but pain and
resentment ... I felt that I had indeed compromised something about
myself in getting a PhD. I blamed myself for 'throwing away' a
relationship. I could not believe that I too had gone the way of so many
women whose husbands feel threatened by their learning and go off to
find someone young to mentor afresh. But now, at a greater distance,
I know that the PhD allowed me to make a journey of which I was
immensely proud ... The pay-off now comes through how I can express
the impact of so much personal and professional learning in my life
now — far more fully than I could possibly have done if I had remained
with my husband.

These positive feelings for a project which has been so personally costly
provide the strongest, if also the most poignant, evidence of its meaningfulness.

Chapter Five

The Touch of Passion

As a prelude to his own account of doing PhD research, Ian offers two quotations. The first is from Rilke: 'You must love the questions themselves' (Rilke, in Maslow, 1966). The second comes from a discussion, by Bogdan and Biklen (1982), of qualitative research: 'However a topic comes to you, whatever it is, it should be important to you. Self- discipline can only take you so far in research. Without a touch of passion you may not have enough to sustain the effort to follow the work to the end, or to go beyond doing the ordinary' (Bogdan and Biklen, 1982).

For all ten students who speak here, their research has personal meaning, personal value. The questions at issue in these projects matter to those who explore them. Towards the topic of their PhDs they stand, not as detached observers, but as people with an existing involvement, an insider's knowledge, seriously committed to taking that knowledge further.

What are the ten topics of this student group? In most cases, their direct personal relevance is immediately apparent. Jocelyn, a Black woman, is concerned with the impact on Black children of positive self-reference material. Qadir, also Black, has as his focus the socialisation of white and ethnic minority young people. Ann seeks in her research to explore the underpinnings of the racism she daily witnesses as headteacher in an inner city school. Another experienced teacher, Sheila, is examining the stresses to which children at school are subject — stresses of which she became acutely aware in her most recent teaching post. Grace's interest in the topic of gambling arises directly out of her own first-hand experience. The existential questions which form Chris' research topic have, as he describes, represented life-long personal issues. For Maggie too, the meaning of reading has deeply personal ramifications, some of which are painful. Susan and Lesley both view the subjects of their research as in some sense representing themselves: in Susan's case, as mature learners, in Lesley's, as working class girls.

Only for Ian was the topic of his PhD, as he originally defined it, a topic from which he stood apart personally. He set out to study personality change in adolescence. It was, in his words, to be a 'hit-and-run exercise in research methods', within which the 'hypothetical entities of self-concept and self-esteem were more important than the subjects', and measurement 'did not take into account what the person themselves thought about what was happening to them'. Not long into his research he moved to a job involving the rehabilitation of head-injured people and he decided to explore the question of personality change within this group. Doing so brought about a fundamental reorientation towards his subjects. Instead of being 'inter-changeable', as the members of his adolescent sample had seemed, the brain-injured people with whom he worked closely became 'unique individuals worthy of study.' This radically altered the character of his research. 'Rather than being an exercise in research methods, it became a way of allowing people to speak themselves about their changes.'

This change in his own position brought for Ian, in turn, a sense of the deep, if often difficult, personal meaningfulness of what he was doing in his research:

> My research isn't important to anyone else. As far as academic impact is concerned it's only a small brick in the wall. Extremely trivial and 'academic'. But for me personally and for my own development as a human being and an observer of human behaviour it is vitally important. I suppose the journey is the all-important thing. As Stevenson observed, 'To travel hopefully is a better thing than to arrive, and the true success is to labour.' To prolong this metaphor I suppose that this way corresponds to hitch-hiking a journey. Not quite knowing where you are going and when you are going to arrive. Conventional research is like making a journey you know by public transport. It's fairly reliable but it can be pretty boring. My research seems to be like walking in an unknown foreign country. Slow, full of surprises, but above all a very different learning experience. Again, this is not the scientific impact but the impact on me as a person.

Ian's story is of a change of direction in the course of his research — a change which brought with it a radical personal reorientation. And perhaps real research, if it is more than what Ian calls a hit-and-run exercise, must always entail personally significant kinds of change. What may, at the start of a project, seem a cut-and-dried sort of undertaking, will, it is certain, evolve over time into something far less tidy and encapsulated. Many of these students, in talking about their work, use the metaphor of a journey. Because they embody real-life concerns, these projects necessarily undergo change and development. Human lives themselves do not stand still and, as several people remark, the meaning of the topic tends to alter as time goes on.

For Ann, whose research issues are closely linked with long-standing professional concerns, new directions in her teaching career brought new perspectives on the topic. As she relates, she began working as a class teacher in 1975, then became deputy head of an infants' school, staying another year in the classroom. Following this she moved out of the classroom, working for the next three years with classes throughout the school, and deputising for the headteacher. In 1985 she took a new job as head of an infants' school in Tower Hamlets, East London, and four years later, another headship of a primary school, again in East London. All these changes had inevitable consequences for the research she had undertaken.

> The work centres round the issues of inequality caused by race, gender and class. Originally I was concerned with how the effects of racism create an inequality in the classroom. ... With the job changes my position changed ... my concerns changed to issues of management. The issues of stressed children throughout an inner city school: recruitment, retention and support of staff — teaching and non-teaching: of community involvement; of whole school development across the curriculum; these became my issues. The centre of my research as I had known it ... had been about the perceptions and effects of racism in young children. This now became *one* of the issues I had to deal with instead of *the* issue.

Ann's dilemma is that of a researcher whose research is prone to its own disconcerting movement. Rooted as the project is in her day-to-day work, its character changes with her changing professional responsibilities. Her earlier crystallisation of the topic dissolves; its focus becomes unmanageably broad. She finds herself needing to redefine issues which are now too diffuse.

Ann's situation is parallelled in some ways by that of Qadir. He pursues essentially the same concerns both in his project and in his professional work. For Qadir as for Ann, this can bring its own difficulties. In his case the daily demands of his job as Race Relations Officer tend to take precedence over the needs of his research. The fact that both work and project are directed at anti-racist objectives does not necessarily make for economy of effort; not is it helpful for Qadir that he uses many of the same methods for the two spheres:

> I use action research a lot in my profession ... and there has been urgency to complete the work and defer the project work ... For years I have regularly done a great deal of pen-pushing. In one way it is good and helps me develop skills but it's very exhausting and takes the charm away from writing for the project.

Qadir's position as a researcher is also like Ann's in that his project has undergone certain major changes of direction as a result of his own professional involvement in its topic. As he remarks, the whole socio-political situation of ethnic minority groups in Britain has radically altered over the past decade; and this change could not but be reflected in the research of someone like himself, who has been professionally active in the field.

Qadir's project grew, initially, out of a previous, smaller project for a Masters degree:

> Looking at differential political socialisation patterns of school pupils of Pakistani origin compared with white British pupils, I found that their perception of the workings of various British institutions and their knowledge of systems did vary, though they were educated in the same classroom, etc. With regard to settlement of 'immigrants' of New Commonwealth origin, Britain was going through an Assimilationist phase, when there was a great deal of emphasis on English language tuition and giving information to the 'immigrants' about the working of the British institutions to 'solve the immigrants' problems'.

> Naturally at the time, my hypotheses were also based on the assimilationist tendency and assumptions, i.e. comparatively the political socialisation of Pakistanis in Britain was 'inadequate (cognitively) and deviant (socially)'. I was able to prove this point ... (But) inevitably political socialisation of Black and ethnic minorities will be different because they go through different experience vis-á-vis racism, ethnicisation and biculturalism.

A few years later:

> Britain nationally had abandoned the quest to promote the concept of the 'flattening process of assimilation' and we were getting on to the Multicultural phase, when there was general recognition that Britain was a multicultural, pluralistic society and that racial minorities have the right to live their cultures and follow their religions.

Later still, when multiculturalism came to be replaced by anti-racism:

> The emphasis of my research has also moved from an assimilationist standpoint through the multicultural to an anti-racist stance. The Black perspective which was 'inadequate' and 'deviant' at one stage has now gained a legitimate grounding from a Black and white anti-racist viewpoint.

As Qadir remarks, his current position is one which makes sense to the Black people with whom he is in daily contact:

> The people basically who have been involved with me, who have influenced me literally on a daily basis, are on the one hand the Black

people generally, their experiences in Britain, and on the other hand the treatment of Black people by British society at large, its systems and institutions, the police, the judiciary, the education system, the housing authorities.

The larger socio-political changes to which Qadir refers are not merely a kind of back-drop to his research; he himself has played some part, in his own corner, in bringing them about. He has, as he says, worked in the promoting of race equality 'on a more than full-time basis' since 1976, and 'long before that, on a voluntary basis.' During that time 'I could notice changes in thinking, in attitudes, in policies and practices as a direct result of whatever little work I was able to do'.

The topic on which Sheila works, as a full-time research student, was not one which she personally initiated. She applied for a funded research post in which the topic was pre-defined; the project was to examine pupils' perceptions of stress in school. But for Sheila this topic proved viable only because she was able to translate its topic into certain long-standing concerns which she had experienced as a teacher, and to bring to it some very personal and hard-won insights and sympathies. Though the project began as something externally defined, proceeding from someone else's idea, in the course of carrying it through, Sheila transmuted it into something distinctively her own.

My background is in secondary school teaching. For ten years I worked for the Inner London Education Authority as a teacher of Physical Education and Human Biology. During that time I became increasingly involved with Personal, Social and Health Education, Community Work and Work Experience. The approach to these subjects is more individual and less didactic than that of general classroom teaching. Indeed, success is dependent on the ability, or perhaps willingness, of teachers to enter into and build up a cooperative working relationship in which pupils' ideas are given as much consideration as those of the teacher. It soon became apparent that involvement with these areas of education allowed me to see facets of the pupils which the teaching of a subject for public examination did not. I was enabled to see the pupils as individuals rather than just faces in a class, names on the register. Many seemed to blossom, to show enhanced self-esteem, to demonstrate a sense of responsibility hitherto unknown and to describe the personal relevance of the work for them.

In 1984 I was seconded for one year to study for an MSc in Health Education at King's College. At the end of that time I returned to teaching but to a different school ... As a result of the time spent out of school I was able to take a fresh look at myself as a teacher and to question many of my taken-for-granted views on education. The new school in which I was teaching had lost its Counsellor in the reorganisation and, perhaps because my new post was mainly concerned with Careers Education and Guidance as well as Community Work, my office became a drop-in place for a variety of young people. Some wanted to chat, others needed to be listened to; some came and went without my ever knowing why they had come in; still others were troubled and disaffected with school.

From talking with, but more especially from listening to, these young people, I learned how isolated so many felt from the process of learning, how irrelevant so much that went on in school was to their way of life. Problems were not confined to the less academic or disillusioned pupils. Success brought its own difficulties for those whose peers were less well motivated.

It is this experience which shapes and colours Sheila's work on the stress which secondary school pupils perceive in their school lives.

In some sense, Ann, Qadir and Sheila all retain a daily concern with the topic of their doctoral studies. In rather a different way, this is also true for Chris. The same imaginative struggles which constitute his research topic also underpin the therapeutic work in which he is engaged. In both spheres, Chris is concerned to resist the pressures of 'normalisation' and to widen existential space. Here is his account of what this topic means within his research:

As Polanyi suggests, our theoretical frameworks — both formal and informal — may be seen as 'mental dwelling places'. Even when dwelling within scientific frameworks, we 'attend to the world' from a centre of consciousness within ourselves; we still have to make sense of these, 'read off' from them, and reconstruct them for ourselves. At different times, say, in different decades, certain frameworks are in the ascendant, become heavily subscribed to and therefore strongly validated. Such sedimentation may lead to a 'hardening of the categories' and when this happens our horizons become narrowed down and potentially 'normalised'. Especially so if we find ourselves within consensual reality bubbles which may powerfully converge our constructions ... If, then, we acknowledge that we find ourselves within a world of multiple realities, we may need to stretch our imaginations and develop frameworks which at least go some way to taking these into account. This may not be easy but it can be interesting and even exciting. From such wider perspectives we may then explore and try to develop methods which describe, operationalise or map, aspects which are more manifest to us — the actual nitty-gritty of doing the research. In so doing we are bringing forth pictures from a vaster multiplicity.

For Chris, the integration of his research topic with his own work as a therapist has acted to validate his doctoral efforts. Feeling that his research concerns have proved fruitful in practice, he sees his studies as having a wider significance than a merely academic one:

> I came to the position that the project might not be accepted for an MPhil or a PhD. But as long as I personally felt in practice the framework and constructions developed had some use in describing and explaining aspects of human experiencing, it was worthwhile. For *in practice,* these ideas seemed to work within the realm of psychotherapy counselling, supervision and facilitation within various training and teaching contexts. I hoped, and still do, that eventually the project will be accepted as a PhD, for I can envisage many further implications deriving from it but even if it is not, by now I feel that I will not have 'totally wasted my time'. This is perhaps an important 'key' to choosing a project. If we are able to choose a project which, even if it were to 'fail', we feel would ultimately be worthwhile because it contributes something to human understanding *in ongoing practice*, then we may have chosen something of value.

For Grace, who works as a clinical psychologist, the topic of her research stands at a tangent to her other work. But her personal involvement in the gambling, and the inside knowledge she brings to it, are no less than for people researching in the sphere of their professional work. Grace defines her relation to her topic in an autobiographical sketch:

> I come from Hong Kong where gambling is an acceptable social activity. Every Saturday afternoon and Wednesday evening, work routines and life styles 'go slow' because people are very involved with gambling: putting on their bets, watching TV or listening to the radio or having time off to go to the races. Throughout my childhood and adolescence I remembered everyone talking about gambling: horses, dog racing or mahjong (a card game). My parents gambled with friends and relatives on mahjong at weekends and at parties. Whenever there was typhoon, people were 'stuck' at their homes and they would play mahjong as a pastime. When I left home and came to live in Kent in 1969, the few Chinese friends I met would often get together to play mahjong or go to the casinos. For the first time in my life I wanted to belong to this group and be accepted by them, so I learned to gamble. That was the beginning of my gambling life. I felt mesmerised by the Casino atmosphere, I enjoyed the carefree evenings with free food and I felt excited when I placed my bets on the roulette table, hoping to win. I have won small amounts and have lost a lot. I would have liked to gamble more but could not afford to.

It was this experience of Grace's that inspired her PhD research: 'I wanted to talk to more gamblers, to find out what they thought and said about gambling'. Nevertheless, it was some time before she was able to 'own' her personal involvement in the topic and to use this involvement as a source of strength rather than something to be denied. With this gradual reorientation, she says,

> I began to feel at ease with myself when I attended their G.A. meetings, and took on more commitment to my research. I became part of 'it' and 'it' was part of me. I sat back and heard what the gamblers said. I was no longer an outsider looking in but an insider looking out.

The real importance for Grace of the topic she is examining provides the essential dynamic in the difficult struggles which research entails. In different terms, this is also acknowledged by Qadir and Maggie.

'Choice of my topic', writes Qadir, 'definitely has something to do with my ethnic background ... My research project has become an integral part of 'me', while I am at work, at home, watching TV or reading a newspaper. Whether or not I have been able to complete the project, I live the project.'

In Maggie's case, the impetus for her research into reading development came from a sense of personal outrage:

> I felt that experimental psychology had failed miserably to deliver anything that made sense to teachers who have the daily responsibility of teaching young children to read. I also felt angry at the way anxious parents had been misled into thinking that there were almost magical solutions for children who were having difficulty learning to read. So little of the so-called experts' knowledge seemed to make sense — it meant taking the reading process out of all social, emotional and cultural context. Or else the experts took just the bits of knowledge that suited them and ignored the rest.

Because her research is concerned with something she cares deeply about, Maggie feels her project has personal value, for all the problems of this sphere:

> I have invested time, money and energy in my work. I have also committed something very personal which is hard to describe. I think you have to care a lot about your research in order to keep going. Simply to pursue an interest is unlikely to provide sufficient motivation to see you through. It isn't that I think my work will have widespread acclaim and change the world in any way, but the research matters to *me*.

Intimate personal involvement in the research topic can, it is clear, underpin commitment to the work, and fire the researcher's difficult efforts with the 'touch of passion'. Yet in traditional thinking, the topic of research should have minimal connection with the persona of the researcher. Personal experience in the area, a personal stance towards the issues involved, are seen as at best irrelevant, at worst a dangerous source of bias and partiality. As human beings, however, researchers necessarily have involvement in the human issues they explore. Unacknowledged, this involvement may, inadvertently and in subtle ways, influence the direction of work which, paradoxically, is seen as entirely objective. If the subjectivity of the researcher is, on the contrary, made explicit, this by no means leads to sloppy or self-indulgent work. When personal values and personal assumptions towards the topic are honestly acknowledged, subjectivity, previously blind, becomes self-aware and self-critical. Research of this kind is far from being an easy option, because it sets at issue aspects of one's personal viewpoint, one's own lived understanding, not some distantly interesting question. Susan's experience, as she describes it, clearly illustrates this.

Susan's topic is the situation of mature learners, especially mature women learners. This topic had become of increasing concern to her after she herself re-entered the formal education system, following a long detour outside it and a transition from the USA to the British context. Previously a high achiever in the system, 'blinkered', as she says, into taking its assumptions for granted, Susan found herself 'desocialised', unable to accept these assumptions, and feeling discomfort and frustration as a mature student. When she began to interview other mature students, most of whom had failed in, or been failed by, the formal education system, she came to a new perspective on her own experience. It seemed that the disjunctions she had felt, and which many people seemed to accept as inevitable, could not be understood without reference to questions of identity, relationships and power in higher education. This meant that Susan, as she puts it, 'began to revisit my own story from the totally different angle that so many non-traditional students opened up to me.'

The development of such personal kinds of understanding is a far from comfortable process, as Susan describes, but its rewards may be large:

Doing a PhD demands accountability within the public domain: in terms of the researcher's conduct, her attention to validity concerns, and the quality and product of the thesis itself. The paradigm within which I chose to root the study demanded other kinds of accountability: to myself, to those who participated in the study, to my supervisor, to others who participated as supportive challengers and to my examiners. Struggles, contradictions and paradoxes associated with the responsibility of such public accountability, on terms coherent with the paradigm itself and my own values, brought to the surface deep veins of knowing and unresolved personal questions. The writing up process, my confrontation with key themes in the data, and the challenge of critically reflecting on what I was experiencing, brought into question the web of preconceived assumptions with which I began the research. In another paradigm, these assumptions might so easily have been kept at a safe distance and neatly reproduced through a so-called 'objective methodology' and an assumed stance of neutrality in the search of 'Truth out there'. Instead, being true to the journey of the research forced a fundamental re-examination of the validity of my starting premises, woven inextricably with my own story.

Confronting the riddle that connected my personal sphere with the public sphere — the latter being the 'issue' which I was researching — generated a new way of seeing and hearing themes across the data that previously I had unconsciously chosen *not* to see or hear. Perhaps most importantly, exploring this 'riddle' and discovering ways of doing justice to its exploration, led me towards beginning to find my own voice: as a post-positivist researcher, as a writer and as a woman.

Research of this kind does essentially entail personal challenge and demand personal kinds of development. For Jocelyn, the concerns of her PhD related to some of her very earliest personal experiences and reflected insights she had developed, actively but not without personal cost, into her own situation as a Black woman:

My research concerns began and took root when I was a child. Although I did not realise it fully at that time, my childhood concerns were the issues that developed over time and were shaped by my various life experiences, into what became the 'Research Questions'.

I remember asking myself a profound question at the age of four in 'post-colonial' Trinidad when I first started to read. My pride in reading aloud to my teacher was always marred by the puzzling question of 'why do these children look like that?' I could not understand why Dick and Dora had this strange paint on their skin and hair, stemless apples on their cheeks. We were all Black children learning to read from the *Dick and Dora Happy Venture Series*, experiencing our first intimate contact with children being depicted on pages of a book. Yet these children were all white with blue eyes and blond hair. I remained puzzled, especially since I felt none of my teachers offered me a suitable explanation.

Eventually as I reached the age of five I turned to my mother, who seemed to be the only one who not only offered me an explanation but engaged me in an ongoing discussion which, on reflection, was surely the foundation stone for my identity. From the age of five my mother progressively introduced me to history and a variety of cultures through poetry and literature. As she explained slavery, she helped me in understanding why all our school books were white oriented. By the age of seven my perception of self, which was not limited because of my racial and economic grouping, was continually nurtured by my mother, who would say: 'Remember child, the sky is the limit'.

Further steps in her own biography led to a still stronger affirmation of her own identity. As she gradually discovered, Trinidad's 'independence', did not mean instant freedom from economic and cultural chains. She herself, together with a group of her adolescent peers, staged a protest which was to make an impact on the educational curriculum:

> Our curriculum was such that we could draw the maps of England and the United States with our eyes closed, and talk about their economic power with only a mention that the raw materials they used, like sugar cane and bauxite, came from the West Indies. A group of us were approaching our O level exams ... we refused to sit our examinations that year. Importantly we got many parents, teachers and primary schools to join us in lobbying the Minister of Education. The Minister met with us and revealed that plans were afoot to negotiate with the Examining Boards in England for the introduction of West Indian Geography, Literature and History as major O and A level subjects. These changes compensated for the personal cost some of us endured by having to sit our exams a year late.

This experience left Jocelyn with a sense of strong conviction about the development of personal identity:

> I knew that it was vital for elements of self to be reflected and portrayed in the environment ... This semblance and portrayal of self in one's environment was essential in the development of a positive sense of identity.

Many years later, as a teacher and clinical psychologist, Jocelyn encountered a characteristically negative image of self amongst the Black young people she dealt with in further education, therapeutic work and fostering and adoptive care. As part of her own clinical practice, she began using 'positive self-reference material' and found that this had a marked effect on the 'sad sense of hopelessness and lack of zeal' she had observed. This was the basis of her research study.

Lesley, who like Susan and Jocelyn has completed her PhD, also sees her project as having both embodied and developed very deep personal concerns. In the story she tells of her research, the exploration of Preparation for Parenthood was also the development of a highly personal understanding: of how an apparently neutral educational curriculum can form one chain in the oppression of working class women — women such as Lesley herself.

Not until she was thirty-eight and studying for her first degree, did Lesley hear of the Registrar General's classification and learn of her own social class status. She was, she discovered, a member of Social Class 5, by virtue of the small wage earned by her factory worker father. She had, it seemed, briefly entered Social Class 2, as the wife of a high-earning senior manager. However, as a single female working parent, bringing up three children on a wage below the official poverty level, she had fallen back into Class 5, with all its expected concomitant social deprivation.

As a student of Social Science, Lesley began to think about the phenomena of social class.

> There was a suggestion that the condition of social deprivation may not be altogether something that one does to oneself through ignorance or fecklessness. It may not be something inevitable, either passed through the genes of one's SC5 father, through the saliva of an infected SC5 husband, or through some mysterious cyclical social malady. Social deprivation may be some necessary part of a system, related to profit making, resulting in exploitation of an underpaid workforce and used to further the wellbeing of those in control of the workplace.

These developing ideas represented for Lesley not merely an academic understanding but a new stance towards her own personal history. 'Events earlier experienced as hurdles, frustrations, normal human adversities were revealed more clearly as related to my social position as woman and as working class.' Her insights were further developed through a Masters dissertation:

> I chose an apparently straightforward question: does the teaching of Child Development in secondary schools 'make any difference'? I soon found that teaching Child Development is in fact preparation for parenthood taught to less academic (correlates with working class) girls — such as I had been. The idea was to teach them parenting skills, so that the ignorance of their mothers would not be passed on to the daughters, the aim being to break a 'cycle of disadvantage'.

This was the stance which Lesley brought to her PhD study of Preparation for Parenthood. It was a study through which she sought to demonstrate, in the clearest possible way, the social injustice to which working class women are subject and how this injustice may be obscured within an educational rhetoric:

> Preparation for Parenthood as a strategy for averting cycles of deprivation was big time ... and substantial careers were being forged out of it. I needed to expose it, to show exactly how Preparation for Parenthood works, how as a discourse it sets out to demonstrate that the working class, especially mothers, are responsible through their ignorance for failures more justly attributable to social policy.

Looking back on the research, Lesley sees it as having been powered by the strength of her own personal feeling:

I don't think I would have been able to complete a PhD, to see it relentlessly through to its end, if my interest in the topic weren't related in some small way to a sense of outrage. Outrage born of two realisations: one centring on the fact that, along with all the other injustices that families on small incomes have to bear, there is another cynical and ideological exploitation, in the guise of Cycles of Deprivation and Preparation for Parenthood. Another realisation centres on those who perpetrate this ideology: those who are in the main financially secure, male, and who have some hidden agenda which is couched in persuasive, misleading, seductive and emotive terms but is certainly not based on emancipatory ideals.

Testimony, surely, to that touch of passion.

Chapter Six

Methodology: a Crumbly Cake

At first sight, any research project appears to be defined by its topic. *What* is actually being investigated seems to constitute the character of the enquiry. Yet, considered further, *how* the project is conducted, its modes and methodologies, the voice in which it speaks, represent more fundamentally its distinctive contribution. And it is often the 'how' rather than the 'what' of their research which is emphasised by students themselves. Achieving a methodological approach which is consonant with one's own values and concerns typically involves the longest struggle in research work and the deepest kinds of engagement. Susan describes the early phase of her own project:

> I was struggling to find a methodology within which I could locate myself ... to find a way of proceeding that was, on the one hand, appropriate to the issue I wanted to investigate but also one which I could 'own' — which did not fragment the complex whole of my own lived experience and my values as an educator. Although in the early stages I could not have easily articulated such concerns nor accounted for them in a theoretical or paradigmatic framework, I nonetheless *knew* that, for example, I was not capable of adopting a 'stranger' perspective nor of violating certain principles I had come to respect about working with adults as learners in my work.

Susan's efforts to develop appropriate modes for own research led her, inevitably, to opt for a qualitative rather than a quantitative methodology:

> Given the purpose of the research, qualitative methods were the only choice for better understanding the situation of adult learners who return to higher education. In other words, I wanted to map the complexity of their experiences and to develop concepts that would

sensitise educators to what can be at issue when adults learn. I was not interested in proving an hypothesis or generalising results to all adult learners.

The adoption of broadly qualitative methods is in fact a common denominator within this student group. And for no one has this been an easy decision. In every case, their academic training has been in conventional quantitative methodology. This kind of methodology, with its ready-made designs, its standard measures, its available packages of statistical analysis, represents a convenient cafeteria of research choices — or, in another metaphor, an off-the-peg researcher's wardrobe with outfits for every possible kind of enquiry. Rejecting these ready-made choices means opting for something much more difficult, something which demands from the researcher both creativeness and responsibility. This is Maggie's account of her own chosen methodology in studying reading development, and the built-in problems which attend it:

> There are vast tomes in the library devoted to reading research, but most are derived from short sharp experimental manipulations. The credibility gap between this kind of work and the reading process is so great that it reduces the viability to almost nil, in my opinion. So I have decided that I need to use qualitative methodology. I feel very confident that in order to examine the reading process as it develops in young children, I need to observe carefully over as long a period as possible. I have to recognise the part that I play in the process as a participant observer. I have to provide my rigour in terms of questioning what I decide to call evidence and what I record. It's a bit like cutting a crumbly cake. If you don't cut it you can't eat it. But if you are not careful, it falls apart. Finding the right knife and the right place to insert it is impossible. I have to make guesses and take chances. My best try will have to be good enough.

Faced with difficult methodological choices, many students have received some crucial support and encouragement from supervisor, fellow-students and friends. For Ian, at a critical moment:

> The obvious answer was to use a qualitative rather than a quantitative approach. This idea was difficult for me to contemplate, let alone accept, because I would be throwing away all the effort and time I had put into understanding and mastering the quantitative approach. If I were to adopt this new approach, I would be left with no firm ground to stand on. It was a very important breakthrough for me personally but it caused me great problems. I was supported by my supervisor in this and although I believe I could have finished the work in less time using a conventional strategy, I would not have gained so much personally, in understanding.

For Sheila, it was through her involvement in the research group that she discovered the possibilities of qualitative methods:

> My entire reading had been confined to literature dealing with conventional research. For quite some time, I tried to fit my own methodology to the conventional approach, although it clearly did not fit. It was during one of our seminar meetings that I first heard the term 'grounded theory'. I was able to apply some of what I had read in Glaser's (1978) book to my own research. However, the real breakthrough came shortly afterwards, when a member of our group suggested that I read *Naturalistic Enquiry* (Lincoln and Guba, 1985). For the first time since I began the research, I was able to identify with what other authors were saying. I was already conducting my research in many of the ways Lincoln and Guba suggested but had been trying, unsuccessfully, to fit it to the conventional paradigm. To discover that I was not alone gave me the courage to come out of the closet.

Grace also found support within the research group for her own difficult transition from a quantitative to a qualitative approach. Her relative isolation early on, both socially and academically, did not help in this transition:

> I was alienated from my upbringing in quantitative and statistical analysis mode. I opted for qualitative research which was for the better but was a hard struggle. In the present day, methodologies were very often taught in universities and if you were a full-time student, you were able to choose more widely than I was. Being a mature student and a part-timer, I found it harder to spend time in discussing intellectual topics or cross-fertilising ideas which can be achieved through full-time facilities. If you constantly mix in the academic departments, or work in a research-oriented and supportive department motivation and encouragement would make a bigger contribution to your own research. I happened to 'miss the boat' one way or another.

However, the research group offered Grace a sharing of experience:

> Most of us were also trained in the traditional modes of research, testing out hypotheses and so on. When we adopted new ideas and paradigms of human enquiry, we were all undergoing changes for the better. Each of us had a hard personal journey; however some got there faster than me. I had to struggle at times but I confirmed that I felt more at ease with myself having done my research in a different way than how I started. I have come a long way from where I was eight years ago but the journey was made easier with peer group support.

In Lesley's case, friends she had made before embarking on her project had introduced her to ideas and approaches which were to prove critical in the qualitative methodology she later evolved:

It was good to be living in Birmingham at that time: for example, I shared a house with members of the Centre for Contemporary Cultural Studies and, although I felt I understood little of their specialised terminology at the time, they introduced me to different ways of conceptualisation just by including me in conversations over shared cooking and over dinner. It was in Birmingham, in a chance meeting with Jorge Lorrain at a party, that I was introduced to the notion of ideology, which proved very useful in my work. Also in Birmingham, I met Francois Baret, a French student of English literature who was using Foucauldian theory to explore the work of Virginia Woolf.

As Maggie comments, the members of this student group are 'all trying to use qualitative methodology as a reaction against hard-nosed psychology with its blinkered approach'. Freedom from the positivist assumptions which underlie conventional methods — however difficult to achieve — has allowed them a sense of breakthrough to new kinds of understanding. Sheila describes her own experience of a study which kept escaping from the Procrustean bed of methodological convention into which she had tried to force it. Letting it take its own appropriate shape created a kind of intellectual liberation:

Throughout my years as a pupil and student I have always been afraid of 'getting it wrong' and before embarking on my own study I read many recipe books on how to carry out research ... I remember explaining how I could not conduct an interview with a pupil who had cystic fibrosis, although he had specifically asked to talk to me about the stress he suffered in school, because he was not in my sample population so to include him would contaminate my data! Later I came to understand that much of what I had hitherto viewed as problems were, in fact, legitimate ways forward. For example, I had been disconcerted to find that my study was changing and developing in exciting but quite unexpected ways. It was with relief, therefore, that I found that a naturalistic approach is interested in an emergent, rather than a preordinate, design. In addition, I found that a study conducted naturalistically relies on theoretical and purposeful sampling, and that talking with the pupil with cystic fibrosis came into this category. A whole new way of looking at research opened up to me as a result of reading the works of a number of authors interested in the naturalistic approach.

Lesley, too, experienced a major breakthrough when she finally turned her back on conventional ways of analysing the puzzling and intriguing material she had gathered. In her previous Masters study of the same research topic, she had worked within the empiricist tradition, testing a hypothesis by statistical analysis. But when that study was 'put to bed', questions lingered.

To understand her PhD data, Lesley needed a far more thoughtful kind of analysis:

> I needed a framework which would make sense of the contradictions I had revealed, the oppositional viewpoints and the subjective assumptions which seemed to work against the wellbeing of the young women who held them. The key to understanding lay in educational policy and the history of education of girls, and there was no obvious method associated with psychology or sociology which would do the job.
>
> My work was held up for years. There was a period when I wandered around the shelves of the Open University library (near my home) taking any likely book off the shelf, just desperate for ideas.
>
> The turning point came when I abandoned the search for an existing framework and began devising my own. It proved to be the most valuable part of my study and, I believe, a truly valuable contribution to the research community. I developed a method of discourse analysis drawing on semiology, on literature focusing on analysis of political communications, and on the work of Michel Foucault.

Susan also looks back on a completed project. Like Lesley, she feels its essential contribution to have been, in the broadest sense, methodological:

> I know that the PhD allowed me to take a journey about which I am immensely proud. I created a precedent in terms of the presentation and writing up of qualitative research. To the best of my knowledge, no other thesis has been written in 'two voices'. This has come to represent an important breakthrough for those who are reflecting critically on traditional research values and assumptions, and are trying to evolve new ways of being researchers.

As Susan argues, research methodologies are never just about 'methods': any methodology incorporates a philosophy which should extend, not merely across practical investigative choices, relations with subjects or ways of analysing data, but right into the complex ways in which the project is defined and communicated through its write-up. Susan was determined to base her account in the post-positivist world-view which underpinned her project — a world-view which insisted that research should be with, rather than on people:

> It was one thing to gain confidence from this world-view to embark upon a qualitative study in a particular way. Yes, it guided how I developed relationships with 'gatekeepers' and participants in the study: how I made explicit my own preoccupations and starting-points; how I involved them in the analysis and interpretation of data. It was quite another to write up the thesis in a way that made those assumptions live on the page.

In approaching this task, Susan found herself very much on her own.

> Traditional approaches offered little to help me through such dilemmas. For example, academic writing conventions are intended to convey objectivity, through exclusion of any sense of the person of the researcher and the use of the third person. Also, dissertations are meant to be written systematically from the definition of the problem through to the analysis of the results. What of studies that need to be written from the inside out? The kind of study in which I was engaging did not begin with predetermined hypotheses to be refuted or affirmed through a series of rigorously controlled experiments. Nor was the design clearly structured from the beginning. Instead, I began with questions and assumptions born out of experience as the starting point for a journey, with no end point in sight.

Susan finally ended her search for an appropriate writing format with the decision to use two voices:

> The second voice serves as a kind of counterpoint to the chronological story of the thesis provided through the main text of Voice One and, as such, has a number of functions. Through it, I foreshadow developments in my own thinking, arising from critical reflection on my own experience and themes emerging from continued data analysis. I indicate, for example, how something that was not clear at one stage became clearer at another. I also use the second voice to show how my initial explicit assumptions were challenged, changed, elaborated or undermined as a result of my engagement in the study. Through it, I highlight for the reader those times in the research when tacit rather than conscious knowing was determining directions or when blinkers were operating with respect to themes in the data. I also discuss struggles and breakthroughs related to achieving a 'realised level of consciousness'. Finally, I reflect on aspects of my own story as a learner, considering points of consonance and dissonance with themes that emerged from the final analysis, thereby illuminating complexities and contradictions. Through the second voice, therefore, I seek to make visible who I am as the 'human instrument' who was involved in the collection and analysis of data.

Really to follow through the logic of alternative methodologies does, as these accounts illustrate, make large demands on those who choose them. Not merely does an unconventional research stance call for the development of original and creative thinking; it also means going against the grain of much academic practice. This necessarily entails risks and requires courage. Looking back on the early stages of her work, Sheila notes her own timidity, seeing herself as 'too afraid of being exposed as a fake and too lacking in academic courage to question what was going on'. Lesley also experienced a strong pull back to a conventional research stance:

> I had been schooled in empiricist science and the use of simple and well-defined methods and criteria for evaluation. At times I wanted to retire to the safety of conventional methods.

Though she resisted this temptation, she looks back at herself as partly failing in courage:

> While carrying out an unconventional study, I was fainthearted at times. Much of my preparation for the viva was concerned with mustering my arguments for not using conventional psychological theories or methods, depending instead on feminist theory, and developing my own method of discourse analysis. During the viva I found that my faint heart had let me down. The examiners thought that the bits that were really me (the questions, the discourse analysis, the political framework) were acceptable, even excellent, but found the feminist theory (which I had soft-pedalled) too fragile.

For some students, temperamental and other personal factors can act to complicate methodological choices. Such factors underlie a certain ambivalence in Ian's position:

> I originally trained as a mathematics and physics teacher. I changed direction to teach adults general studies, mainly because I could see little of relevance in the school curriculum maths and science for the children I had to teach. I suppose I had already started to realise that what appeared to be purely mechanical logic was not the answer to everything.

Ian is very much aware that he views research, in whatever sphere, as a human rather than a merely mechanical activity:

> The mechanical side of research is covered in many texts describing how to conduct research. What is usually forgotten in these texts is that research is not just a mechanical process. Research is carried out by people. Sometimes the subject of research is people. Even in areas where the research seems far removed from humans, the impact of this knowledge relies on human interpretation.

Yet temperamentally Ian feels himself to be an 'analytical scientist: an empiricist who likes to make his way through life making judgments based on hard facts and logical analysis. From my background I am very much that sort of person'. As he says, 'In previous work, this worked very well for me', but he sees his PhD project as having called for another kind of orientation. 'The particular study I wanted to do relied on my being able to pay more attention to values and feelings of individuals than to facts'. This, in Ian's terms, means a humanistic rather than an analytical-scientific orientation.

Unconventional kinds of methodology often carry quite personal implications. Several of the students here see such methodologies as demanding an explicit acknowledgment of their own place in the research. As Susan puts it, 'Paradigm shifts in the social and natural sciences take account of considerable evidence pointing to the fact that the very act of objectifying alters that which we hope to see.' She argues that this calls for 'explicitness about who I am as a person in relation to the world and in relation to the processes and outcomes of the study.' Yet, as Jocelyn insists, there are people for whom such personal disclosure is altogether inappropriate. For a Black person in a white racist educational system, to speak in the first person as a researcher carries unacceptable risks.

'I did not feel as easy as Susan or Lesley about using my voice.' There were, she writes, aspects of Susan's work and comments 'which I as a Black woman could never use, because of how it would be read and interpreted.' Susan, by contrast, 'had permission as a white woman in a white educational system to use her voice loud and clear.'

Qualitative methodology and the limits of its appropriateness in Jocelyn's research formed a central focus in supervisory encounters:

> Many times I left supervision with one sentence occupying my mind, 'As a white person you see no *risk*, but you are asking me to take too many risks with my person as a Black woman in a white educational structure'. How could a Black person really convey a lifetime of the experience of racism to a white supervisor who, however sympathetic, could never *know* this reality and how this reality affected the risks qualitative research involved. At times that reality for me superseded everything I was doing for that period ... Eventually, I believe we settled for what I felt was a place safe enough from which to speak.

This place was in fact a mixed research design, which had an approximately equal balance between qualitative methods on the one hand and traditional quantitative ones on the other.

Methodological decisions entail coming to terms not only with one's own personal situation, values and beliefs, but also with the whole intellectual ethos which pervades research. Whatever choices are made, some inner accommodation must be reached with the intellectual establishment. One aspect of this involves standing up inwardly to conventional research assumptions and ceasing to be intimidated by 'big name' researchers.

As Chris writes:

> Apart from direct social relationships, there are so many powerful indirect social relationships which may affect us in relation to the particular context of doing an MPhil or PhD. These take the form of the 'professional' media such as journals, training programmes and

conferences, which constitute the general 'discourses' in our field. Students may become somewhat awed by the 'big names' in their discipline or profession, especially those heavily validated within their studies and trainings. However, if we 'deconstruct' this, we discover that these 'big names' are or were 'thrown into existence' as individuals; that they have their own personal autobiography and configurations and that they attempted, for all manner of reasons, to make sense of their 'worlds' and the contexts in which they found themselves. This is not to deny or disparage their achievements but to *relativise* them and to locate their works as potentially useful human constructions with an 'instrumental' range of usefulness.

Many students, Chris suggests, might feel themselves to be above this kind of intellectual intimidation. Yet perhaps everyone embarking on a research project needs to try to gain a perspective on current intellectual fashions and thereby achieve a certain distance from them.

Although initially, upon more intellectually sophisticated levels, we may dismiss this proposal that we can be somewhat overawed by such 'lime-lit' others, it may be worth contemplating 'at other levels' ... try to step back from the whole academic or professional scene and realise its relativity. Read about scientific revolutions, fads or trendy ideas, 'the sociology or philosophy of knowledge' (but beware of ideologies, e.g. Marxist) just to get a relativity in time and culture, not to gain any absolute view. What are the consensual bubbles of reality presently around for you?

The kind of intellectual overview which Chris advocates may enable dogmatic positions to be avoided, and what is valuable in a variety of research methodologies to be recognised. This is something which Maggie feels to be important. She deplores 'the deep divide between academics, which splits departments'. On the one hand, many eminent psychologists will have no truck with qualitative methods, finding 'this style of work, where no statistics can be spewed up and fed into computers for detailed technical weaving, too messy, and consider the work to be without merit.' On the other hand, a radical approach carries potential intolerance: 'The danger is that in one's efforts to justify the movement away from something traditional, you tear down everything.'

In the last analysis, as Maggie points out, all PhD researchers need to acknowledge their own academic context:

We have to recognise that the research cannot be isolated from the real world of departmental boards, external examiners, upgrading hurdles, and the final goal is that other people, whose opinions matter, find your work acceptable.

What is encouraging in the experience of this student group is evidence of increasing liberalisation in the intellectual culture surrounding PhD research. Lesley, found that, so far from being penalised for abandoning a conventional approach, she was taken to task by her examiners for a lack of boldness in justifying her own radical methodology. And Susan experienced an affirmation, at the crucial examination stage, of the risks she had consciously taken:

> The challenges of being accountable to the academic establishment can create all sorts of pressures to compromise oneself. By evolving and then risking a new form, that had integrity for me and cohered with the values, assumptions and process of the research, I managed to get the qualification in ways that I believe took the 'new research paradigm' further.

These outcomes have been noted with pleased surprise by Qadir, who, from what has happened in others' examinations, feels he can now afford to abandon his previous total reliance on quantitative methods:

> I have always been obsessed with the need to satisfy the supervisor or the examiner with regard to the quantitative aspects of the project, until recently, when I have noticed some colleagues completing their project doing a fraction of the quantitative work, compared to what I have done. I have to learn to have faith in submitting a good deal of qualitative data.

From his colleagues' experiences, Qadir's confidence seems justified.

Chapter Seven

Experiencing Supervision

It is because the whole PhD experience seems to rest on a straw that I
need competent and professional supervision.

So writes Maggie, whose own history as a supervisee has involved much
vicissitude.

When I started thinking about doing my research I had no idea what I
would need a supervisor for. I thought that doing research was a
solitary exercise which I would be expected to do almost completely
independently. I think that I expected to show finished chapters to a
supervisor who would make suggestions for minor improvements and
correct my inevitable spelling mistakes and grammatical errors.

I made several appointments to see my first choice supervisor. She is
an expert on children learning to read. She has a deep love for literature
and is always able to make me feel excited about reading. At the start
she was very important influence on me as she was a wonderful
antidote to the dreadful, dry, sick approach to reading which the
majority of psychologists seem to favour.

I duly planned a pilot project and spent a great deal of time reading
stories to very young children. But something started to go wrong. I
couldn't see it at the time but now I think I understand what happened.
I gradually lost confidence in myself under the influence of this
supervisor who did not see my distress although I can remember
choking back real tears at one group session with her. Her style,
academic background and experience were vastly different from mine.
She is an English academic, not a psychologist. Her experience is
largely with reading success, not failure, which is an everyday occur-

rence for me. But it was more than that. I can joke about my poor spelling, I can smile about my sixteen year old son who has never read a book in his life and I can laugh about my husband who once shocked a posh dinner party into silence by admitting that he did not read books. But I felt that my supervisor was leader of a club which I could not join. A couple of her other students admitted to me that they found her overpowering but they coped because they could join her club. So to conclude this sad little episode, I would say that it is more important to have a supervisor who recognises your personal commitment to your research, than to have an expert in your field of study. This could well be the reason why so many research students fail to complete.

Meanwhile my second choice supervisor continued to invite me to join her seminar group, which I enjoyed in a rather distant way. She finally rescued me from my abyss by writing me a pretty straight letter. The gist of this was why the hell did I think I could manage on my own and why didn't I come to see her for regular supervision which, in her experience, students always needed. Since that point I think I have gradually learnt how to use my supervisor to help me. It's not easy. I have to tell her what I need her to do, eg. please remind me that at the end of the month I will write a summary of what I am going to do next. It is almost like using someone to be an extension of oneself. So all the emotions that I feel about my work: eg. guilt about the slow progress, fear of failure, sudden loss of confidence, are felt more acutely during supervision. I don't find it easy to make and keep appointments, I get anxious. But this is the necessary tension which then means I can creep slowly forward after each session. The second supervisor has never let me go away feeling destroyed although I think we would both agree that I still have a very long way to go. The fact that my research is not a special area of expertise for her is of no importance. It is quite obvious to me that if I had only one supervisor, the first one, I would have packed up by now. But the juggling necessary to work with two is impossible. As far as I am concerned I have only one supervisor now.

Being at the receiving end of supervision is, as Maggie's story shows, a far from simple matter. Because the PhD undertaking is so essentially fragile, students can easily become demoralised through the stance taken by others who have an official involvement in it. The apparently most helpful interventions by the apparently most well qualified supervisors can, quite inadvertently, act to undermine rather than enhance the personal confidence which is so fundamental to the carrying through of original research. PhD work is shot through with anxiety and this must inevitably affect the character of supervisory encounters. This forms one theme in the experience of the present group. All ten students, in defining what they value in supervision, mention the importance of emotional support.

Susan describes the vital role for her of personal encouragement, referring to 'the cycles and cycles of vulnerability, in which so many ages and stages of support are required.' A central function for her of the supervision group was the individual, mutually supportive relationship she was able to develop with another member, Jocelyn: 'a relationship that was central to the core of the journey of the research.' Having met through the group,

> we began to explore and enjoy our differences ... learning from each other, questioning, making sense together all the time. And then, in the final stage, I learned that even when you have come this far, you can still give up. But neither she nor (the supervisor) would let me. Each supporting me in different ways.

Grace emphasises how crucial it has been for her that criticism has been constructive, rather than leaving her feeling bad. Both she and Ian mention the supportive function of the group. Grace writes:

> Both the supervisor and my student colleagues have given me unconditional support. Every time I felt utterly unable to complete my chapter, I thought of the 'waiting group' who keep suggesting that there is a goal awaiting that I have to attain, that will need all my effort ... they were all sharing my experiences with job and family stress. We were all from a similar age group; professionally we were all achieving, but we all wanted to develop ourselves.

At times in her work, this group became her 'main lifeline'. For Ian too:

> One of the main sources of inspiration has been the research group ... The social side of research is very important. I have found that a large and active research group is really useful. Rather than being a student working on my own I can share my problems with others. As a research student working on my own or in a small, competitive group I would have missed out on the vital supportive nature of the group.

Chris' account sounds a similar theme:

> I have been fortunate enough to have a supervisor who has genuine concern and empathy for her students, can be constructively critical, and has supported my various — perhaps at times seemingly rather eccentric — 'orbitings'. She also set up a group for the people doing research projects which she was supervising. Again the culture of this group was supportive and although criticisms may arise, these tended to be constructive, an approach that had regard for the person rather than an insensitive machismo blunderbuss approach.

Sheila also emphasises the quality of personal support and compares supervision with therapy:

> Often by the time we meet I am even more riddled with self-doubt about my ability to complete the thesis than at other times. This can frequently be accounted for by the fact that I have reached an impasse, can see no way out and need help. In many ways it takes courage to meet ... I scrutinise her face for signs of exasperation, listen for censure in her tone of voice. It is essential for me to admit my ignorance, reveal my fears and express the many doubts which assail me if I am to benefit fully from our meeting, but this can only be done within a caring, supportive atmosphere. The research is part of me and to share the research means sharing myself. This can not only be risky but also destructive, if entrusted to insensitive people.

That supervision can indeed be destructive is mentioned by several students, drawing on their own experience or that of friends and acquaintances. Maggie's story is one example. Chris warns of supervisors who have no real empathy for the project or understanding of the attempt to construct something new. Such people, he suggests, so far from 'encouraging you and your processes, will try to get you to conform to the intersecting discourses they are plugged into.' This is likely to be particularly disastrous at the incubatory stages of research, and may, in Chris' words, amount to 'symbolic murder'. For Jocelyn, it was precisely at the beginning of her project that she encountered pressures to distort or abandon the directions she wanted to pursue:

> I was determined not to be disillusioned by supervisors who found the topic 'not too hot to handle' ... Deep inside I felt my concern was genuine, the terrain was virtually virgin soil especially in the United Kingdom, and come what may I was going to find a supervisor ... I was rapidly starting to feel like a lonely Black Woman Professional who was being seen as dissatisfied with 'good traditional developmental issues'. One person was actually honest and told me 'Try to get back to the States; you will find the sympathy you're looking for there. As much as I am excited by your ideas I could never take it before the department's research panel.'

Sheila also suffered directly from unhelpful supervision:

> I spent a great deal of time, initially, trying to decide how to approach the study. It took me a full six months to become sufficiently organised and orientated to produce a research proposal. During this time I had great difficulty in communicating with the supervisor whom I had been assigned as part of the studentship package. I compare my experience of her with working on shifting sands. She vacillated; the advice given one day was contradicted, forgotten or denied the next. Although a

most pleasant person socially, I had no confidence in her academically. It is impossible to share hopes and fears, half-formed, perhaps foolish ideas about one's research, with someone for whom one has no professional respect or trust ... It was only after lengthy negotiation that she was persuaded to relinquish her role ... but when she did, the work progressed more smoothly.

Lesley has advice for beginning students that touches on many of the ways in which the supervisory relationship may be a negative rather than a positive force:

During my career as a student I found out that the single most important influence on the progress and outcome of my work was my supervisor. My first bit of advice would be, don't let a supervisor be forced upon you. Before you confirm who your supervisor will be, make enquiries of other students and get some background information. 'Getting on' with someone is crucial. I have seen 'not getting on' with a supervisor lead to a long drawn out and painful disaster: a failed PhD and a demoralised student.

Most of the ingredients of 'getting on' are simple and the naive might assume them to be easily available. It is essential to find someone you are likely to like and trust and, if possible, someone who already likes and trusts you. Find someone who is interested in your area of study and thinks it is worthwhile, not someone who keeps a stable of researchers working on areas which are satellites of their own interests ... if your study begins to turn up results which threaten your supervisor's theories, what then? Find someone who will not seek to 'collect' your research and ideas to enhance his or her own reputation. Find someone who is not limited in the range of theory, research methods and techniques they think are acceptable. As you get deeper into your study, you may find your ideas and therefore your methods and theory changing, and you should not be strait-jacketed by the limitations of your supervisor.

Find out about the style of supervision: for example, avoid someone who tends to be controlling and didactic. Avoid anyone who makes you feel small, weak or supplicant. Supervisors are inescapably in a power position; some work hard to avoid taking advantage of this, some do not.

Practical things assume immense importance. A supervisor who goes off on holiday, a lecture tour or worse still, retires at a crucial time in your research, can have a devastating effect; good supervisors will give you plenty of notice of their availability so that you can organise your programme of work accordingly. When feedback is essential, for example on a written chapter before proceeding further, you need to know feedback will be forthcoming within a reasonable time. Students I have known wait fruitless weeks or months for feedback, by which time either their ideas have moved on and the feedback is useless, or they have lost touch with their research and have to waste many hours locating the threads again. Meetings with your supervisor are important: find out if your supervisor takes times and dates seriously. I have heard from many fellow students that, while some supervisors might not break a social engagement without ringing first, it is quite possible for a student to turn up for an appointment only to be told by a secretary that the supervisor is not available. Don't take these things for granted as common politeness, make enquiries among existing students before committing yourself to sharing their supervisor.

Lesley adds a note about her own strategy:

I personally didn't carry out enquiries like these — I went by a seat-of-the-pants 'getting on' feeling. I stood by this feeling, however, against a great deal of pressure to take a supervisor from the university where I was employed. As it turned out, I learned the essential ingredients of 'getting on' from my long, deeply satisfying experience of working in the student-supervisor relationship.

Her outline of what this has entailed conveys the importance of practical aspects.

Supervision was, over the whole period, entirely positive. There was a felicitous pattern. First the appointment, always at a time convenient to someone travelling long distances, between the end of the working day and just before a group meeting so as to minimise the journeys required. I would send written work well beforehand; in early years it would be a working paper, a new perspective I was testing, new methodology under development. In the middle it would be techniques for organising data and early results of analysis. Towards the end it was drafts of chapters — there were many drafts before the point of completion was reached. Moments of crisis received instant and serious attention. While sometimes I left a session with a lot of rethinking, reading and reworking to do, there was always the feeling that this was a positive development and not a period of going back and starting again.

As Lesley suggests, the dimension of power is inevitably present in student-supervisor relationships. Many of the bad supervisory practices she describes can be seen as proceeding from the unthinking misuse by supervisors of such power. The exploitation of student work to build one's own empire, the messages of personal superiority, the low priority given to students' urgent needs, the casual treatment of arrangements — all these derive from gross inequality in the respective positions of those involved. If some supervisors unconsciously convey a profound disrespect for student projects, this is no more than a living out of a situation in which the position, and the undertakings, of a PhD student can command vastly less interest, less weight, less authority, than those of a lecturer in an established academic post. Political considerations are seldom recognised in the discussion of academic life, where the discourse of scholarship and rationality tends to preclude the acknowledgement of power dynamics — as witness the difficulties met by those who struggle to raise consciousness of race, class and gender issues in the world of higher education. That academic power is seldom made explicit can create real problems for students.

The position of PhD students is itself particularly ambiguous and fraught with difficulty. Ostensibly, those who are engaged in work for the degree of doctorate rank high in the academic hierarchy. They have proved themselves intellectually, by gaining not merely first degrees — and good ones at that — but also higher, Masters level qualifications. Far more than for students studying on taught courses, their studies require a high degree of intellectual autonomy. They must establish their own frame of reference, define and pursue their own curriculum, make their own decisions about the methods they will use, even, to some extent, decide the criteria on which their work should be assessed.

Yet against this high academic status stand certain features which place PhD students at the bottom of the pecking order or altogether outside the hierarchy. One such feature is the relatively small economic contribution they make. This is because their fees are low compared with those of students on taught courses and also because, through the way academic funds are allocated, their presence brings only slight financial benefits to the academic institutions in which they work. PhD students occupy a position which can command very few rights. Unlike those studying for first degrees, they have no staff time officially allocated to the support and development of their work but are instead dependent on the personal priorities — or the personal caprices — of their supervisors. This puts them in the role of humble petitioner, rather than of academic colleague whose proven accomplishments may sometimes even outshine those of their supervisor.

Inevitably, this complicated situation must in some sense affect every student-supervisor relationship. In one way or another it forms a strand in the experience of many of the students speaking here. Ann, for instance, reacted with anger, dismay and personal doubt to the whole mystifying aura with which the academic world is invested:

> I remember two interviews we had — and here comes the honesty bit — I was terrified and felt I was without academic skills and knowledge. I wasn't only terrified — I was overawed and at a loss. I was scared to say what I didn't know ... But why out of my depth? In my early seminars I didn't understand what was going on and this confusion was at several levels — and caused several responses within me:

inadequacy, ignorance, anger, confusion, rebellion and excitement — logic tells me that this list contains important dynamics for an individual — there is within it the danger that being incapacitated too far would lead to complete withdrawal from the whole situation.

What didn't I understand in early seminars? At one level the actual words being used by members of the group. One that has stayed with me is Academe. I had never consciously heard the word spoken before — I knew what it meant — I hadn't known how to pronounce it. There were other, more complicated things being said about individuals' research of which I knew nothing — the anger in me came from ignorance and the assumption that we all understood. I was too scared of looking stupid to ask what the words meant. I also felt that if I stayed with it I would know what they meant: I, too, would become clever — it had to be catching and I wanted the germs.

It took time and work on both sides before Ann was able to establish a different and more appropriate stance towards her situation. The felt inequality of the student-supervisor relationship gradually dissolved into something very different, in which Ann's irreverent humour is never far away. And, as she describes, her position within the supervisory group became transformed:

As time went on I acquired enormous respect for the group — I came to see it as a refuge — there I didn't have to fight — politically I am in tune with people. If some members are more Left than I, I feel only admiration. It was this that made me feel I was a member of this very moral group. That became the privilege and the honour — not that I would become clever! This belonging has made me fight harder for equality, for people's rights; it has widened my perspective on issues of inequality and limited resources — it has caused me to want to investigate the structure of society and its class system.

In a different way, Sheila also suffered a painful sense of her own lowly status as a PhD student, with no right to expect any real interest, let alone personal commitment, from those with established positions in the academic world. In this account she addresses me directly:

My study was really still in its infancy at this stage and I so very much needed to talk to someone, to try my ideas on someone, to risk sounding like a fool with someone, to be reassured and told that the few embryonic ideas I had could develop into a full-term PhD thesis. Because of all the supervisory trouble I had experienced I did not feel I dared reveal my insecurities and doubts to anyone. I did not think that anyone at college was strong enough, capable enough or even interested enough to cope with them. (She describes contacting someone who suggested she should get in touch with me.) This I tried to do, although it took an enormous amount of courage. What would this very good, highly respected lady who was an expert on Kelly ... make of me who, if the truth be told, knew little about Kelly other than his name? I rang the Institute but you were not there. Anna Brett was helpful in the extreme; I gave her my message and she took my telephone number and said that she would ask you to ring me. She sounded so positive that I almost believed her. When I thought about it for a while I realised that I would never hear from you ... But you were an exception and you did return the call.

Sheila goes on to describe her doubts, after we had met:

> You said that I might contact you at any time ... For some time I was rather reluctant to make appointments to see you and give you work to read because I felt that, as I was getting something for nothing, I had little right to it and was afraid of taking advantage of your generosity. I know that you explained many times that you were interested in the research but somehow I could not fully accept that. It was only after you approached me several times with your diary in your hand and your pen poised to write in our appointment that I fully appreciated the genuineness of your original offer to contact you at any time.

As with Ann, Sheila came to adopt a much more confident stance towards her own situation as a supervisee:

> Having overcome my initial reluctance to contact you, I soon began to see you as 'my supervisor' ... I always give you my work to read first. When you return it, I feel excited and cannot wait to open it and see what you have had to say. I instantly set about working on any amendments you suggest. There is something psychologically satisfying in tidying up the work and feeling that it is finished.

The accounts by Ann and Sheila show how hard it is to believe in the value of one's work within the closeted world of academia which, through its apparent lack of interest and respect, seems dismissive of it. But conversely, the experience of many students bears testimony to the helpfulness of supervision which succeeds in reworking the built-in academic inequalities which underlie these messages.

As Lesley suggests, supervisory relationships, if they are to be facilitative, need to be two-way: to involve *mutual* trust, *mutual* respect. Research entails authorship, and the personal context in which it is conducted has to acknowledge and foster student autonomy. This is not to deny that supervisors have a particular kind of authority which students do not possess. By virtue of their acquaintance with the academic frame of reference in which higher degrees are conducted, supervisors serve an essential advisory function. Their knowledge of the scope, organisation and presentation required for

PhD work is vital, particularly at early and late stages of projects. But these aspects stand apart from the fundamental processes involved in doing original research, and here it is the students who possess authority. The responsibility for formulating issues, defining directions, deciding upon modes, belongs to the student, not the supervisor.

One aspect of respect for student autonomy is the preparedness to make room for and encourage perspectives that are different from the supervisor's own. For the two Black students in the group this aspect, not surprisingly, has been particularly salient. Jocelyn comments:

> The journey with my main supervisor has not only made an indelible impression on my thesis but on my life and how I approach my work and writing now. Journeying to a place of mutual respect, empathy, clarity and success for us as a Black researcher and a White supervisor is worth writing about ... aspects of that journey could be crucial for other Black researchers on that lonely research track in White institutions.

Qadir's account expresses similar concerns:

> I have had no problem in conveying my 'feeling' vis-á-vis my project. When researching into the 'plight of Blacks', Black students have always suspected 'white academic supervisors' for not taking the same side. But I have always found (his supervisor) with me on an anti-racist stand. Perhaps it is her involvement in supervising a variety of projects to do with gender, race, class and disability which is indicative of her empathy to these perspectives.

A recurring theme in the comments of these students is the value of supervision which contains and encourages the project rather than seeking to direct it. Helpful supervisors are seen to establish a psychological space in which student creativity can flourish. In Maggie's experience it was recognition of her own personal commitment, as against eminence in the field of study itself, which proved critically important. As she remarks:

> Originally I thought I needed academic support or stimulation from a kind of mentor. But this is very far from the truth. An academic mentor can only lead a research student along a well-trodden path. It takes a different sort of mentor to encourage a student to take risks, to follow hunches and to hang on to the passionate interest that started the whole exercise in the first place.

Jocelyn's first supervisory encounter was crucial; as she says, 'I realised that here I could negotiate.' For Ian too, it matters that supervisors and their groups give students the initiative:

> In the group I belong to the supervisor often takes a non-directive role and is not the centre of attention nor the guru around whose feet the

research students sit waiting for the pearls of wisdom ... The role of the academic in lectures and tutorials is often as information giver. Many, I feel, are not practised or interested in the role of facilitator nor in the other roles which supervision requires. The supervisor may see that their role is in giving answers rather than helping research students find their own solutions. The supervisor needs to be an open and confident person who can let others be the centre of attention where this is necessary.

Both Lesley and Sheila comment on the value of supervisory relationships in which their own autonomy is affirmed and encouraged. Lesley describes her supervisor as having 'at no time led or blocked my ideas, but she has at all times facilitated and made them possible ... Long before I thought of applying to do a PhD, she indicated that she had no doubt that I was capable of completing one, and I grew into the idea through her confidence in me.'

Sheila tells of how her confidence regularly returns in supervisory sessions:

> ...as I begin to see new directions in which to move. It is essential to make clear that the new directions are of my own choosing and not suggestions from (her supervisor). Never does she tell me to do this or not to do that. From her questioning and probing I am encouraged to explore and articulate my unexamined motives, my taken-for-granted assumptions about the research ... I am enabled to reformulate my ideas and see new angles of approach. By this time I usually experience a renewed sense of excitement about the research. This undoubtedly results from the fact that I have chosen the next steps — they, therefore, have personal meaning and resonance for me.

Susan's account of being supervised stresses the importance, for the development of her own creativity as a researcher, of her supervisor's challenging, sometimes even confrontational approach:

> From the beginning, she challenged, always pushing my boundaries, moving me towards regions that often threatened. Challenging me to be reflexive about myself as a researcher and where and who I was in relation to the research. To find my own voice and express it. To show explicitly how I was being challenged and changed through the journey of the research. Helped me to understand from the inside out, a key validity concern in qualitative research ... If she had merely 'facilitated' me, been responsive to my needs, I could not have learned as much as I did, nor would I have had such courage to push back my boundaries. Challenged me to move beyond my own givenness. And in ways that involved the whole of me, not merely my intellect.

Good supervisory relationships emerge from these students' accounts, as being mutual, personally intimate — and adventurous. Those involved work together as colleagues, as partners, rather than as superior and inferior kinds of academic. In the context of such relationships, projects proceed through understandings hammered out together; but in these understandings, it is students' promptings, students' feelings, which are paramount. However, within this general consensus that student-supervisor dealings need to be collaborative, speaks one dissenting voice: that of Qadir. His comments must serve as a qualifying footnote to these conclusions. Commenting ruefully on the 'lenient nature' of his supervisor, he wistfully imagines a more authoritarian approach: 'Had she used her whip, which she never did, I would have, I am sure, responded.'

One aspect of the supervisory function which these students have experienced is the use of *ad hoc*, semi-structured group exercises. For all who comment on them, these exercises have been personally valued. Both Chris and Lesley emphasise the importance of the lack of structure, in enabling them to draw upon deeper levels of awareness than are generally accessible. Chris writes:

> I have always got something from the experiential sessions which allows me to focus upon aspects of research. I also feel the occasional unstructured session allows things to emerge, even out of a certain quietness at beginnings.

For Lesley, the absence of structure 'creates a different atmosphere, relaxes protocol, deepens communications, allows expression of half-formed thoughts.' She goes on to show how, for her, the play-like character of these exercises is personally liberating:

> They free me from constraints of 'reality', e.g. being polite, being rational/logical, being serious/adult, so that I am able to think laterally — more creatively — and so that I can explore issues unencumbered with preconceptions.

To begin with, however, the informality of these occasions and their abandonment of the usual conventions of academic talk, can be personally disconcerting. Grace describes her own early reactions:

> When I was first given the exercise, it often puzzled me. It appeared to me a difficult question/action or even at first glance quite difficult to organise my thoughts about what to do, what to think or how on earth can we do it? Once the initial panic passed, the thoughts circled round, and somehow something surfaced. Usually thoughts emerged. The internal focus came forward; the problems that had been bothering me had a chance to stand up. Very often the thoughts which were then put into action or words in the exercise, could highlight a few answers or give me positive strategies or understanding of some kind.

A theme within the comments of several students is that this kind of activity offers a safe space for personal exploration. Sheila writes:

> Taking part in the exercises put flesh on the dry bones of the theory; they give life to what had seemed somewhat abstract and brought out the 'personal' ... This was reinforced by the variety of our approaches to the same exercise. They helped me to clarify my thoughts in a non-threatening way because there were no right or wrong answers. Through discussion in twos or threes an original response could always be modified or extended in a supportive atmosphere ... I always felt able to express my feelings and doubts (something I rarely do in a group) because each person's contribution was seen as valuable and there was never any pressure to say the 'right thing'.

That many people did indeed make use of the opportunities to take things further, through these activities, is clear from several accounts. Here is Jocelyn describing her experience of one exercise:

> In a small group of three we each had to take on the role of someone in our research. After giving a brief synopsis of the person chosen and the situation, the rest of the group directed questions to that 'person'. ... We all found this an extremely enlightening exercise. For myself, I had the experience of 'being' a particular teacher whom I felt was delaying the Action Research Project in the school. It was only when I was asked questions and had to answer like 'him' that I really could appreciate the journey he was undertaking. This new perspective made me more understanding and sympathetic and definitely contributed to the way I interact with the staff team and how I now present the research.

Another exercise, mentioned by both Grace and Susan, entailed using group sculpture to portray the place of the research project within the student's life. For Grace, this task 'revealed the reality and problems in juggling with my work, family, research and self ... and created space and insight to reflect on how much time I allowed my research into my life.' Susan, who found such exercises both 'useful and powerful', describes the use to which she put this particular one:

> We were asked to sculpt where the research was in our lives. Merely having time and space to reflect on this was helpful. But then, by translating these reflections into physical representations of my life, in terms of relationships, work demands and other commitments, I was far more able to confront the risks of it becoming marginalised. I began to conceptualise where some of my difficulties lay, and in turn to consider, with the help of the group, what kinds of action I might take to shift certain patterns that were unsatisfactory.

One exercise undertaken by the group involved pairs of people working together: each asked the other that person's most dreaded oral examination question. Paradoxically, this task, ostensibly focused on something negative, served for those who engaged with it an essentially positive and confirming function. To Grace, the exercise 'gave me confidence in handling examination questions' and offered 'the amazing discovery that we were worried about similar questions.' For Jocelyn and Susan, the task brought a sense of affirmation. As Jocelyn describes her experience:

> Many of us realised that our fears and feelings of inadequacy were projected unrealistically onto the questions. However that was useful because, like others, I realised that many of the fears were unfounded ... What was even more interesting was the fact that this exercise, simple as it appeared, actually assisted me further to assert my affirmation and belief in my research.

Susan writes of a similarly positive experience:

> This (exercise) helped us to see how what we most dread can afford the greatest possibilities for showing our strengths. By anticipating experientially, I experienced affirmation, as well as sharpening up the ways in which I might approach challenging questions.

Susan adds that; 'talking about such matters would not have been nearly so effective.'

This aspect of supervision entails a group of supervisees; and the character of the group, as several people remark, is fundamental to its value, even its viability. Most obviously, these exercises involve sharing with others features of research which are seldom discussed, may be hard to convey and may carry difficult feelings. Several people in this group speak of the pleasure and the relief of being able to engage in this kind of sharing. Sheila's previously quoted remark expresses her sense of personal freedom within the context of a non-judgmental and supportive group. Grace describes feeling personally reassured by the discovery that others have similar anxieties. For Lesley, an important function of such exercises is that they act to establish positive social feelings within the group: 'they create bonding between differently-thinking people where only differences were apparent before.'

Ultimately, it is the personal dynamics of the supervisory group which, as Grace and Susan both point out, will govern how much may be achieved by these kinds of experiential exercise. In the case of this group, the exercises were only possible, writes Grace, 'because the group *trusted* each other, there were no fears or competition.' For Susan too, trust is fundamental; she goes on, however, to mention the vital importance, in such delicate kinds of group work, of respect for personal privacy:

Significant learning for me always entails risk taking and learning through doing, in a learning climate characterised by support and genuine dialogue. The exercises, therefore, do not occur in a vacuum. We experience them within a nexus of particular relationships in which the trust required to become fully engaged as a whole person, rather than merely a cognitive self, has been developed ... Within our group there is a tremendous amount of trust between each of us and our supervisor. Within the group itself, this varies. The value of these activities is often very personal, but there are also opportunities to follow up the learning with (the supervisor) and with others. Group discussion is always helpful. But each time, you find your own level within it, and your privacy and that level of engagement is respected. This, I believe, is critical.

Chapter Eight

Managing

PhD work, it is clear, is no easy option. The intrinsic problems of carrying through an original piece of research are apt to be complicated by circumstantial difficulties. Every student must face the question of how to fit a major research project into a life filled with other commitments. Beyond the problems of competing claims on time, energies and resources, there are also issues of personal management. With no external structures to support and guide research, in emotional or practical ways, each person must find their own mode of managing the work. Since PhDs have by definition no precedent for those who undertake them, the situation is necessarily a new one, with no prior experience to draw on. Through often painful trial and error, false starts and unattained resolutions, PhD students have to achieve for themselves the complex and delicate task of forging a personally viable mode of working.

> For me, writes Grace, life became a juggling act. Most of the time I managed to keep the three balls in the air (work, family and self) but now and again it fell apart because of particular demands like illness in the family and work promotion. My research became the victim and I reverted back to keeping up with daily demands, forgetting my commitment to myself and my research. When work and home placed more demands upon me, I felt angry with myself as well as others, with my guilt and a host of mixed up complaints like the stress of being a woman with an expected role in society. There were marital difficulties, conflict between personal struggle for freedom and ties to the traditional world I lived in.
>
> To complicate matters, I had a difficult relationship with my boss. Lastly, I was my own enemy, because I took a long time to overcome

self-doubts, my fear of failure and my sense of inadequacy in writing and doing a PhD.

The personally complicated situation within which Grace conducts her research is characteristic also of other students in this group. A common feature is a feeling of pressure from conflicting commitments. How do people deal with this problem? Among the students here, different individuals have arrived at particular, sometimes contrasting adjustments. Like Grace, Jocelyn felt herself torn apart — between her project on the one hand and her very young baby on the other:

> I have since wondered if the joy experienced in touching the carefully bound thesis could ever compensate for the balancing act of priorities that the process of the research demanded. The sacrifice at first involved guilt around having too little time for my baby who was actually only six weeks old when I started. The main part of my guilt rested there because I steeled myself not to allow friends and family to increase that guilt whenever I could not participate in invited events. Balancing that scale so that my daughter and my thesis each received the right amount of attention was at times a nightmare.

Two features proved critical for Jocelyn in resolving this personal anguish. One of these was the concept of 'quality time':

> This concept changed everything; time, however short or long, was going to be utilised to its fullest. I then started introducing 'my daughter and my thesis' to this concept. I was amazed how my daughter accepted and grew over the years with the concept, so much so that the concept of quality time is still used in our household, actually enriching our relationship.

The other key for Jocelyn was her decision to adhere strictly to a tight schedule for her project. With her young baby and a demanding full-time job, she could of course devote only a part of her time to her research, but...

> the thesis behaved like a naughty child. At first it refused to accept that I could only attend to it part-time. I was determined to resolve this and I succeeded in doing so via stringent Work Plans. My first Work Plan charted me to complete the thesis in four years part-time. I was convinced I could do it. Furthermore, unknown to all at first, was the fact that this time scale helped remove any remaining guilt around time for my daughter. Every morning I promised myself that I had to finish this thesis before she was five years old so that I could be fully focused on her as she advanced to the primary stage in her education. Thus structuring my time input into thesis and family helped towards what resulted in success at both ends. In four years and three months, as a part-time student, I had my thesis completed, bound and submitted.

My daughter was also happy and we thrive on a powerful relationship with my even having extra time with her before her fifth birthday. I now advise anyone undertaking this journey of the PhD to structure your time, time-scales and events as much as possible — even if the method may appear clinical, it works.

What works for one person may not necessarily suit another. Maggie operates a different strategy in dealing with the competing claims of project, work and family. Rather than trying to stick to a preordained, set timetable, she adapts in an *ad hoc* way to demands which arise unexpectedly: 'I have learnt to be pragmatic; when family or work pressures take over the allotted time, that's life.' Grace too has a relatively open view of time, seeing the completion of the project as more crucial than the number of years it may take:

> The long term goal and the responsibility of finishing the research was an important landmark. It did not really matter whether it was five years or ten years; but the nearer I was to the deadline, the more committed I felt towards finishing the project.

One aspect of Grace's position derives from her sense of personal priorities. Insisting on an early completion of her thesis might entail a price she is not prepared to pay; she would rather give the project, for the moment, a lower priority:

> I found ways of coping in coexistence, by leaving my own research in the least urgent pile. It will get there eventually, a matter of more years and a matter of having to 'wait'. I have asked myself what is the urgent need: if I have finished my research but lost my children or my husband, would I be better off? Wouldn't it be better if I have helped my children to achieve, kept a family together and eventually achieved my own goal in my own time?

For no one is a PhD their only undertaking in life. Somehow research must be fitted in with domestic and family responsibilities — and, for most people, with paid employment too. Maggie, for all her capacity to adapt to unforeseen exigencies, sees herself as needing actively to clear spaces for her own research — particularly, to limit work demands:

> I am struggling with myself to try to prioritise the time needed to finish the work. With an enormous heave, I could finish in three months of solid working. But I can't have three months, so somehow I have to withdraw from my work commitments in some way and claw out some time. There's no earthly use my thinking that I can fit it into my leisure time. I have become obsessed with sailing and I love our garden. While I frequently allow peripheral things to obtrude into my study time, setting aside time is paramount.

If full-time work inevitably conflicts with the need for research time, some kinds of job are perhaps particularly difficult to manage alongside a PhD project. Qadir has some suggestions for beginning students, borne out of his own hard experience:

> One should try to get a job which is undoubtedly relevant and complementary but not interfering. In my case, for years I have regularly done a great deal of pen-pushing. In one way it is good and helps me develop skills but it is very exhausting and takes the charm off writing for the project. Do not take on any other research projects. Sadly in my case, I used action research a lot in my profession which was not *directly* related to my project, and there was pressure to complete other work and defer the project work. I believe single-mindedness is crucial; it is essential not to be distracted.

Given the pressure of so many competing commitments, it is hardly surprising that these students are much preoccupied with time. This is not just a matter of struggling to find enough of it. There are also difficult questions as to how to achieve an appropriate structure for the time that is available. One problem is that the part-time character of most PhD work renders it highly vulnerable to interruption. As Ian remarks:

> This type of project, because of its long time-scale, interferes with personal (and family and work) time in such a way that the threads of ideas are continually interrupted. Research like this appears very much a two steps forward one step backward sensation.

Qadir sees this situation as calling for regular and sustained attention to the project:

> One needs concentrated spells, to do some justice to any creative and original work. Therefore it will not help to leave work open for weeks at the same page and return to the same point, time and again, never having long enough to resolve it and move on.

Grace has arrived at similar conclusions:

> The time commitment and continuation of time, that is, a few hours every day, was better than a block of one week every month. The problem with that was the interrupted thought patterns, particularly when I was stuck. It was easy to forget about it but that became a recurrent time-wasting pattern for the next six months, before I felt the energy to do something about the blockage.

For most people in this group, progress along a time-scale is both uneven and unpredictable. Unusually, Jocelyn's use of time has been planned and executed with great deliberation and precision. She describes here how she came to structure her personal schedule, following a group exercise:

I consider myself a very disciplined person, and as such my plan of work for each year was judiciously done and assessed periodically during the year for target completion. However, I felt I needed to do something more as I approached completion but I was stuck. (The supervisor) calmly stated that our exercise that evening would require each person to map chronologically the process of a goal 'from now to completion'. I had just started the laborious task of 'writing and rewriting' so I decided that my goal should be completion of the PhD. I shall never forget the experience of charting month by month the tasks I wanted to accomplish. I remember so vividly how loudly my heart beat when I reached the ninth month and I realised that if I followed my plan, within a year I should be completed. I remember a few smiles from some in the group whose eyes told me this was 'wishful thinking'. My head was reeling, I was choked with excitement. I drove home and immediately went to work on carefully breaking down each goal into its working parts. Next day I placed the structured plan on a Wall Planer and a small Filofax Year Planner. Now I was surrounded by my Work Plan right up to completion and I ticked in red each completed task per month. Thanks to this task, my journey to the finish line was clearly planned and judiciously followed.

Asked what is the major obstacle in PhD work, most students would probably cite time. The perpetual shortage of time, the lack of hours in the day for study, the encroachment of other things into the precious small space reserved for the project — all this seems to constitute the most essentially difficult aspect of carrying out research. Yet, as Sheila can testify, the fundamental problems are not simply those of time. Unlike the other students in this group, Sheila conducts her study on a full-time basis; she has, as she says, 'all the time in the world' for her project. But this apparently privileged situation brings its own difficulties. For one thing, being a full-time student makes for passivity and procrastination:

> I seem to have lost that great sense of urgency I had when I was studying part-time for my first degree. Nowadays I frequently put off until tomorrow what I am having problems with today. As a part-time student it was not possible to do that; problems had to be wrestled with as they arose, otherwise work would never have been finished.

Sheila finds it particularly difficult to set limits:

> I am in danger of operating as if the research were a full-time 'real' job. I could quite easily get caught up in the process and forget that there is actually an end product. With all written work there comes a time when the student must say that the effort is 'good enough' and finish with it. However, as a result of having so much time, I frequently spend ages drafting and redrafting whole sections, changing a word

here and rephrasing a sentence there. I recognise that this can become a displacement exercise, especially when I am unable or unwilling to apply myself to a new section. Were I a part-time student, there would simply not be the time for such refinements.

Perhaps the most serious problem for someone doing a full-time PhD is that of having to stew in one's own juice when the work goes badly. At such moments one comes face to face with oneself. There is no getting away from the frustration, the guilt, the self-blame, the sense of failure. This situation can be utterly debilitating.

The gift of unlimited time is a luxury and, when the work is going well, I very much appreciate my good fortune. However, during the dry periods when my mind seems totally empty, I long for the legitimate escape into the demands of paid employment. But I have no such bolt-hole and cannot justifiably seek satisfaction in another sphere. During the barren times I can feel so tired that I sometimes wonder if there is something physically wrong with me. Some days I feel ready for a nap around 10.30 a.m. but have not yet given into the temptation, although on some cold, wet, miserable winter afternoons I have allowed myself to have forty winks! On these occasions I wonder if I shall ever cope with a full-time 'proper' job again, if this is all the stamina I have!

Doing a PhD means managing oneself: in some sense, students *are* their projects. For everyone, the long time-scale of original research proves emotionally very uneven. Inspiration is notoriously erratic and cannot be summoned at will. Rare moments of elation are likely to be outnumbered by periods of doubt, frustration, dreariness or lack of direction. How do students cope with such fluctuating emotions? How do they sustain their own inner purpose and resolve at the times they simply feel like giving it all up? For some people, it is a question of keeping a firm hold on what is positive in the work. Qadir finds 'it is important to "capture the inspiration".'

Grace reminds herself of her own motivation for the undertaking:

Self-determination that I was doing research work for self-development, personal growth as well as professional development. I had to stop waiting for my husband or family to be ready to give me help, I had to get on without any further delay.

In order to sustain this ongoing motivation, Grace has found that she needs to be very careful about the demands she makes of herself:

Realistic goal setting is an essential criterion, in order to avoid subsequent feelings of inadequacy. I have learned that I had to set small steps and achieve those steps, however small, in order to reinforce myself in feeling positive about continuing my task.

Sheila, too, has come to evolve a strategy for keeping herself going:

> I have found that it is essential to write — to write anything at all and to keep writing. It is no good (for me anyway) to wait until I am inspired. That way nothing would get done.

An important part of the difficult task of sustaining autonomous personal work is that of developing for oneself practical ways of organising it. Most basically, this entails questions of physical space. Maggie comments 'I have found that having a private space in our busy family house is essential.' And Grace writes of 'the very basic of finding myself a *desk* in a room where all my papers are not to be moved because I may not go there for a few months in a row.' At another level, as every student has found, it is crucial to evolve some way of organising and systematising the work. Without this, there can be only chaos, as Qadir knows from bitter experience:

> I regret that I have not documented enough in a manner useful for my project. It is mostly relevant but scattered and needs collecting together. Moreover, I have read a lot and still continue to do so but I have not developed a system to document literature. I have tended to create *corners* and *piles*, which are growing as the time passes and becoming unmanageable.

The necessity of organisation was also learned the hard way by Lesley:

> As my research got into full swing, I began to develop a system of organising the information that I was finding and generating. If I had started with this, I would have saved months, perhaps years.

In achieving a viable and personally appropriate organisational system for research, categorisation is the key. In dealing with references, for example, Sheila classifies them by broad topic:

> All my cards are 5 x 8 inches. I have three labelled and differently coloured boxes, one containing cards on research into stress, another containing cards on research methodology and a third containing cards on personal construct psychology.

She also classifies and keeps all the notes she has made within separate containers:

> I keep *all* (and I mean all!) notes in box files. Nothing will be thrown away until I have successfully completed the thesis. I have a different box file (two in some cases) to each chapter and contained therein are the may drafts I have made of each section of each chapter.

Lesley uses a similar indexing system but it allows for cross-referencing:

> I keep a box file, where I store ideas, notions, theories, arranged in alphabetical order. Some notions require several cards, 'Ideology'

started off with a brief note but grew to occupy almost a file of its own, as I uncovered its long history and changes of emphasis. These files cross-reference with one another.

PhD study extends over years. Not surprisingly, these students share a preoccupation: how not to lose vital parts of the work. In particular, as several people note, it is fatal to rely on memory. A book or article which formed a major landmark early on — something which it would apparently be impossible ever to forget — turns out, at the writing-up stage, to be entirely untraceable. Through her comprehensive recording system, Sheila has been determined to guard against such disasters:

> I keep a note of *all* books and journals I have consulted even if I have not used them in the writing of my thesis. It is as essential to keep a record of 'dead ends' as it is of constructive leads, otherwise one may find oneself down the same dead end again and even again. For this I use a card system on which I write the title, author, publishing company and year of publication. Additionally, I note the library from which I have borrowed the book and, most importantly, the library shelf mark, which saves a great deal of time should I need to consult the book again. When taking notes from a book which has been edited, it is essential to write down the title of the chapter and the author as well as the title of the book, the editor etc. as this saves time when collecting the references. If a book has been especially relevant, I make a photocopy of its reference section so that I can do some follow-up reading. At the end of each chapter I have made a point of ensuring that I have all necessary references whilst they are still quite fresh in my mind, before embarking on the next chapter. I have learned from my mistakes to make a note of everything (well almost everything!) that I think may be needed. It is foolish to imagine that I will remember where I found this, that and the other.

Given the erratic way in which creative work proceeds, PhD students need to allow for the unexpected, to take advantage of serendipitous discoveries and encounters. 'Be prepared' is one of Lesley's principles:

> When I go to libraries, bookshops and visit friends with large book collections, I take a stack of six inch index cards in an elastic band. A small notebook and pencil in a pocket is often useful and beats collecting and then losing scraps of paper, envelopes and the inner core of loo rolls upon which are scrawled essential but indecipherable notes. One regularly meets people, even or most often at parties, who have come across that elusive reference which will solve the current problem, or will introduce to the one other person working in the same area as you, or who in conversation changes your life. I was in my tightest denims for a party in Birmingham when I met Jorge Lorrain, a refugee

from Chile who had just written a book on Ideology. This was a felicitous introduction to a notion that was to provide the turning point in my analysis. It was about that time that a notebook small enough to fit into the back pocket of my jeans became an essential item of dress. Don't forget the pencil — by the time you ask around and find something to write with, your informant has moved on to the *vol au vent*.

Nor is it only the ideas and the work of others that PhD students need to document. As Sheila insists, comprehensively recording the details of one's own fieldwork can be just as vital. Without this, crucial aspects of the research may be lost forever.

Throughout my fieldwork I kept a very detailed diary which included information about the weather, how I felt physically, emotionally and psychologically. I noted down such facts as my arriving at the school soaking wet and spending an uncomfortable morning because my feet never dried, or sitting in a room which was too hot or too cold. I recorded both good and bad feelings in myself; how I perceived staff and pupils and how I perceived their perceptions of me and how these changed over time. I made notes on the people I had spoken with as soon as possible afterwards, and recorded how I considered the trans-actions had gone. No detail was too trivial for me to jot down and I certainly would not care for some of those involved to read what I wrote about them! Undoubtedly my scribblings were subjective but they were absolutely vital when the time came for me to analyse the data. Analysing the data, for me, was much more than just listening to tape recordings and allocating slots to the various utterances of the pupils. It involved my getting back into the situations, reliving them and seeing and hearing the people again (very often, I should like to think, in a more insightful way), watching their actions and very often hearing in quite a different way what I thought I had heard on the tape. I certainly could not have done this without my extensive notes.

As Sheila's comments suggest, research work may generate very large amounts of material. The question arises of how to store it all. Nearly every student in this group has invested in a computer. For most, this has meant acquiring operating skills. This can be problematic, as Grace has found: 'Finding myself a word processor, and storing the information on 'hard disk' for over two or three years, can be a headache.' However, the learning has generally paid off. Chris remarks 'Once got used to, a word processor eases things, e.g. mistakes, swapping things around. This can save hours of work in the future.' For Maggie, too, 'learning to use first the BBC word processor and now the Apple Mac, has been pretty important. I am learning to assemble notes, start new files and sort them and to keep references as I write.'

Simply having a computer does not guarantee protection against disasters. Amongst PhD students a particular nightmare sometimes recurs: vital work will somehow get lost. Having suffered this trauma, in reality, Sheila has some cautionary remarks:

> From the start I was aware that I should keep a copy of my work on a back-up disk in case of accidents. However, perhaps as with plague, famine, war and terminal illnesses, we like to imagine that they happen to other people but never to ourselves. It was only after I lost a whole week's work, which simply disappeared from a disk that I now make not only one but three back-up disks of each chapter.

Epilogue:

Being a Supervisor

The position taken by academic staff towards their students must bear some relation to their own experience as undergraduates and postgraduates. When I look back to my own student days, I see my undergraduate studies as having in the main failed miserably to live up to the high hopes and expectations I had of them. But in the desert of dreary lectures and boring, difficult laboratory work, there was one brilliant and luminous strand: James Drever's course on perception. Once a week, on a Monday morning, something quite different happened in the lecture hall of the Edinburgh Old Quad. During these sessions Drever offered us the very material with which he himself was struggling, the extraordinary discoveries that were then coming from the work of Ivo Köhler. These discoveries, as Drever made us see, called for nothing less than a total reconstruction of ordinary human realities. But what emerged from his lectures was not a finished product. The ideas he sought to express had no ready formulations, and were visibly difficult to put into words. Drever was in any case a deeply shy man, driven to communicate only by his own sense of the significance of what he saw. Yet because he spoke from the place where he was actually dwelling, spoke of what he was at that moment stirred by, what he felt to be of momentous importance for psychology — all this meant that for us as students it became possible to engage with material that was living, and to feel involved and enthralled in the subject we were studying.

After my first degree, I went into clinical work and did not resume academic studies until I registered for a part- time PhD five years later. I think my motives for undertaking a doctorate were mixed but they included an obscure sense that the topic — conformity — had a personal significance which I needed to understand more fully. Over the six years I worked on

113

the project, my involvement in it was very uneven. It was not until the stage of writing it all up that I came to feel that it was *mine*.

This happened rather mysteriously. Though I had not consciously attended to the deeper meaning of the work until the final phase, when I did so I found that the topic itself had somehow changed; questions of conformity had resolved themselves into questions of a larger sort, involving love. Without my apparently having thought about it, I seemed to have come to a kind of personal conviction, a position towards the issues I had been concerned with. The empirical material I had gathered had, of course, prompted and informed these developments. But it was only when I actually sat down to write the thesis that it became possible for me to explore my own assumptions in the light of this material, and to find out what I really now believed. This entailed a definition of my own frame of reference, whereby what had previously belonged 'out there' in Psychology with a capital P, became something I could actually, excitingly, own for myself.

My experience as a PhD student had little to do with any official supervision. The man whom I approached, as someone holding both clinical and academic posts, was perfectly frank about the conditions under which he would agree to act as my supervisor. Only if I would undertake to see him no more than once a year, and then merely to report progress, was he willing to undertake the nominal role. Frightening though this contract seemed at first, the arrangement proved in fact to suit my own way of working. But this was, I am sure, because throughout the years of my PhD work I had the constant personal support and affirmation of my close friend and colleague, Don Bannister. Because I found it hard, while I was working on the project, to say what it was about, I did not actually tell Don much about what I was doing. But I was aware of his firm belief in my capabilities, his conviction that I would carry through what I had undertaken. Had my official supervisor, whose orientation as a behaviourist was very different from my own, chosen to intervene in the ongoing work, I think this would have killed the project off; such was my sense, until the final stage, of the tentativeness of my own venture.

I believe that what I offer as a supervisor is grounded in my own experiences. If my supervisory practice is mostly positive, it is because I can convey what I have learned for myself: the importance of trusting in one's own struggle for meaning, the courage to live with uncertainty and to resist quick and facile answers, the refusal to be intimidated by important names and the weight of reputable publications. But because all this is very personal, it is not possible to communicate it to everyone. Only where there is a mutual respect, a sense of reciprocal resonance with the other person's ways of seeing things, can these kinds of messages be conveyed. With students whose seriousness I can feel, whose projects clearly carry personal depth and urgency, I feel confident in undertaking supervision. Conversely, if on their side there is a sense of empathy with my approach, the relationship is likely to be fruitful. However irrelevant, even dubious, such aspects are conventionally supposed to be, I have learned to my cost that it is fatal to disregard, on either side, these personal feelings.

Though my own experience as a PhD student taught me about the importance of research as a process as well as a product, it was some years before I began fully to follow through the logic of this realisation. Towards the first project which I supervised, I adopted a broadly traditional role, seeing my responsibilities as advising and criticising within a context of deliberate personal distance from the student. Well- organised, enterprising and resourceful, the student himself politely accepted this kind of supervision, successfully completing the thesis within the expected time. Yet in the following years, he remained deeply dissatisfied with the work he had done, feeling that he had failed to engage with the underlying issues, merely skating superficially over them and not doing justice to his real concerns. As I later came to see things, my own failure to encourage and support this student's personal commitment to the work had contributed to its limitedness.

Some years after this, when I took up a new academic post, I inherited two ongoing PhD students whose supervisor had retired when they were both in the midst of their studies. The inadvertent loss of someone with whom the project has been negotiated from the start, to whom its rationale and methodology make sense and who is committed to seeing it through — this loss, for most students, is catastrophic. And so it proved for one of these students. Our ways of posing questions, our stances as researchers, our approaches to psychological meaning were mutually antipathetic. Try as I would to disguise my differences as a psychologist, to support the student in her chosen line of research, things nevertheless fell apart and, after more than 12 years of working on the project, she finally abandoned it.

With the other student, however, things turned out differently. Somehow she managed to convey to a new supervisor who had not been in on the birth of the project, what it was that she was trying to do. She did so in such a way as to convey its depth of personal meaning, and to allow my own real engagement with it. Given the circumstances, this student's successful completion was a personal triumph.

Another student whom I undertook to supervise was an apparently pleasant and conscientious person who brought evidence of high academic ability. Nonetheless, there was something about his research approach which made me feel very uncomfortable. Unwisely, I ignored these feelings. It was not until we had been working together for two years that it became obvious that his interest in his young women subjects was a prurient one. At this point I withdrew from a supervisory role which I should never have taken on.

For different reasons, supervision also broke down in the case of another student. Here I failed to realise that the student wanted a far more directive kind of relationship and that she was particularly unhappy with the personal openness of the supervisory group. In retrospect, I wonder at my own slowness in 'reading' her frequent non-attendances and missed appointments. Finally she found the courage to express her alienation and her decision to withdraw her registration. I was left with a sense of partial responsibility for her three years of uncompleted work.

I have also experienced wholly positive ways in which my supervisees have decided to abandon their research projects. In two cases it has become clear, as the work progressed, that the student's essentially practical aims would be more appropriately pursued by more direct forms of action. It has not seemed, in these situations, that the two or three years of PhD studies have been a wasted effort; in both cases it had needed this kind of exploratory work to articulate personal goals which were previously obscure.

My unhappiest supervisory experience, without doubt, has been with a student who took her thesis to completion but then failed. Looking back, I see disaster as having been built into the situation at several levels. She was jointly supervised by myself and a colleague whose orientation was diametrically opposite to my own. This shared role was chosen by the student herself, who felt that she would benefit from opposite and therefore complementary approaches to research. Predictably, the reality turned out to be very different from this happy anticipation, and left the student feeling torn between irreconcilable choices. The thesis she submitted — a compromise between two kinds of research — was referred for major rewriting. Having substantially reworked it, she was again referred, this time by a different panel of examiners who were out of sympathy with the first. At this point the student, about to take up a new teaching post in another part of the country, abandoned the whole project with understandable bitterness.

Reflecting on this experience, I see other fundamental reasons for the student's failure. It was, I think, a misjudgment on my part and that of my co-supervisor to allow her to register when she did. She was in fact the prototype of the supposedly ideal PhD student. She was in her early twenties, had just completed her Masters course in the institute where she intended to register and, as a full-time research student, seemed likely to attract an ESRC studentship. Typically for someone in that situation, she proposed for her project an extension of the work she had done for her Masters dissertation. Because I had supervised that dissertation, she asked me act as one of her PhD supervisors and I — too readily, as I now see — agreed. As the work progressed, it became more and more evident that this student was not able to move beyond derivative formulations. Though academically competent and conscientious, she lacked the intellectual and personal maturity needed for original work. And for anyone whose first-hand experience has been that of recipient, whose life contexts have been educational institutions, it is perhaps almost impossible to have evolved a personally distinctive position towards life. To me this student's tragedy spells out the importance, for PhD research, of personal maturity.

In my own supervisory history, unhappy outcomes such as this are greatly outnumbered by success stories: of students who are awarded doctorates. Quite often these doctorates have come from difficult, even apparently unpromising beginnings. Several students have, months and even years into their research, rejected the approach they had been following, seeing it as compromising their own values or beliefs. Yet in no case has this meant throwing out the baby with the bath water. Overcoming the temptation to abandon the project altogether, each of these people has found the inner strength and courage to begin afresh. The resulting theses have, in my judgment, been all the finer for the waywardness of their course. Painful and costly as the thinking behind them has been, the final products have carried personal weight and conviction.

For most students I have supervised, the process of PhD work has entailed a long and difficult inner struggle. Typically this has meant a struggle with deep-rooted feelings of personal limits and personal inadequacy: the belief that in the end one is unequal to this ambitious task. Women, in my experience, are particularly liable to suffer this persistent inner self-depreciation; given the gendered power structure of the social world, including that of academic institutions, this is hardly surprising. With many of the students I have known, these feelings have acted temporarily to sabotage their confidence and stop them in the tracks of their ongoing work. At such moments my own genuine conviction in the value of their research enterprise, my sense of the unique contribution they have to make, has I think been very important. All these students have in fact taken their work to successful completion. And paradoxically, the self-doubts which have formed part of the backcloth to the research process have added to its final value, in ensuring scrupulous care towards the work and an unpretentious honesty of approach.

Some of the most exciting theses I have supervised have been the outcome of the most prolonged and complicated journeys, involving eight or nine years of work and many vicissitudes. Often this is because the student moves out of a conventional, positivistic, pseudo-scientific research mould into an approach which is daringly personal. In two cases this happened when the student chose to come to me from another institution, where supervision had disallowed this kind of movement. As in all such supervisory changes, this shift made for great difficulty. Real personal concerns have had to be extricated from a design which stifled or excluded them. Both students happened to be people of strong convictions and high personal integrity. And again the final form of their work has carried all the greater weight through the personal struggle and determination that has gone into it.

Many of my supervisees have taken a long time to believe that their own ideas could matter: that they could actually put themselves into what they were doing. When at last they come to acknowledge their own personal commitment, involvement and responsibility in the work, the research becomes transformed. In place of dead, bleached-out abstractions, of hollow, unconvincing generalities, speaks a truly human voice, offering living material.

Most fundamentally, I think, supervising entails relationship, and what essentially defines that relationship is trust on both sides. Without trust the relationship cannot be established. If I am to encourage and support a personal enquiry, I must genuinely respect the person concerned and believe in the work they are undertaking. It is equally vital that the student trust me: my capacity to listen and to hear their concerns, my having no hidden agenda, my real commitment to seeing the project, as *their* project, through. If the supervisory relationship works well, mutual trust continues to develop and deepen as the project work progresses. But in my experience this development is not generally smooth or easy. One reason for this is that PhD supervision does not happen in a vacuum. Most students have long experience of academic relationships which are basically authoritarian. Their present context is often within a department whose culture and practice may be at variance with genuine openness and collaboration. All this cannot but have its effect. Into the privacy of a tutorial in my office intrude academic messages of a different kind. One fine day a student with whom I have worked closely over several years, to our mutual satisfaction, abruptly and unexpectedly casts me into an altogether alien role. I have become for the moment the representative of all that is worst in academia. What I am actually saying seems to count for nothing. I stand, in the student's eyes, for a particularly narrow, prescriptive, even punitive approach to research.

I find this experience quite painful, no matter how often it happens; it calls into question what has seemed to be a well-established basis for working together. Sometimes it proves fairly easy to dissociate myself from this role but sometimes I seem to remain stuck with it over the course of several meetings. Eventually, of course, in shared reflection on some aspect of the project, the student does 'hear' what I say. The working through of such an episode seems to make for a firmer sense of mutual trust — although this is no guarantee that it will not happen again.

One aspect of institutional life in education is its heavy emphasis on production. The traditional assessment of learning has as its criterion the essay or the written exam paper. What has gone into these products, the modes through which they have come into being, are considered altogether irrelevant, of no consequence. Viewing learning as a process worthy of respect means going entirely against the grain. And nearly every PhD student, in my experience, has assimilated all too well the conventional ways of appraising their own learning. 'I'm not ready to come and see you yet, I haven't written anything since our last meeting'. How many times have I heard this! In this situation I find it very difficult to convince people that, as I believe, it is the times *between* producing field data or writing that are the most important in doing research. Again there is often a sense of frustration, of beating one's head against a brick wall, in trying to convey a message which students are, inevitably, so reluctant to believe.

The kind of supervision I try to practice can often make for a bumpy ride. One major reason for this is that insisting on the value of prolonged reflection and the avoidance of cut-and-dried solutions imposes personal discomfort on student and supervisor alike, and puts a strain on their relationship. When the student's forward thinking seems to have failed or the project to have reached an impasse, I feel huge pressures to step in, to offer helpful advice about the directions which might be taken. This betrayal of respect for the work would, in the short term, allow us both to breathe a great sigh of relief. Refusing to take this line means prolonging a difficult and uncomfortable period from which we would both be glad to escape.

In all PhD work, a critically important and necessarily difficult time for both student and supervisor is the stage of writing up. It is the written thesis which will form the focus of examination, and it is the thesis which will act to communicate the whole import of the work. Yet, in my experience, nearly every student at this stage underestimates the effort to be made, and as a result may need to rewrite, perhaps many times over. A metaphor which I think captures the problem of this phase is of completing a complicated piece of knitting. After many months you have at last finished all the component parts: beginning by redoing the first section to get the tension right, having at times to undo and rework the difficult pattern, enduring an anxious time when the shop ran out of the original shade of wool, finding that the last 'little bit', the border, involved far more work than you had ever expected. But now at last, having finished, all you have to do is just sew it together. Yet as I have learned from bitter experience, the task of assembling the knitted pieces for a garment demands every bit as great an effort as went into the knitting itself. Hastily cobbled together, the beautiful, painstaking work looks lumpy and unattractive; it is something no one would want to wear. All the months of effort have, it seems, been entirely wasted.

Just like knitters impatient to be finished, the students with whom I have worked have nearly all tended to truncate the difficult and lengthy process of writing up, thereby selling short all the efforts that have gone into the work. Of course there are many obvious reasons why this should be so. Most students work part-time on their theses and may have little continuous time and space for this phase. Sometimes they are concurrently engaged in a job hunt, in which having obtained a doctorate might make a critical difference. Many students feel a strong sense, by this stage, of having spent so many years on the work that they can allow themselves no more. And few people adequately anticipate the sheer difficulty of writing up: of transforming into coherent and sequential form the whole complex, wayward and chaotic process of a research project.

All this makes for a less than adequate account of the work that has been done. And this is where there must often be a struggle in the supervisory relationship. Since to me it is absolutely vital that the written thesis does justice to the research, I view myself as the repository, the guardian of the student's own highest standards. I do, therefore, set out to be as carefully, scrupulously critical of the write-up as I can: its style, its content, its structure, its inner logic. This period of supervision is often very fraught.

Writing is an extremely personal matter, and it is necessary to approach with tact and delicacy. Yet even so, to urge reformulations can produce anguish or hostility. Among my supervisees, however, no one has actually followed through their threats to abandon the work. The write-up has, through the student's commitment and courage, become fruitfully revised — and the relationship has survived.

When a PhD is awarded, the supervisor is often congratulated. Speaking for myself, I do feel a sense of triumph and joy when this happens. It is very important that there should be a public acknowledgement, an institutional recognition of serious personal enquiry. In the award of the degree lies a valuation of the long, lonely, difficult struggle, the periods of doubt and despair, which original research entails. Projects which I have supervised are certainly not my work. Yet though they are not mine, I have had a great investment in them and I have come to care for the people whose work they are. Because of this, I felt relief when regulations in my own university precluded the appointment of supervisors as examiners. I had found the role of examiner of my own supervisees nearly impossible, so difficult was it to achieve the necessary distance from the project.

I think the conventional image of supervision is one of conferring of benefits on supervisees. In my experience the gifts are definitely two-way. For me, working with PhD students allows a mode in which I feel personally comfortable, and which I believe enables real learning to occur. Academic teaching on formally assessed courses imposes a strait-jacket; it constrains me as 'the expert' — a position which is personally alien. In supervising someone engaged in their own line of work, I am free to speak from my own real experience, to offer what I can in support of a project in which I believe. I have intimate and privileged access to a unique intellectual journey, to the excitement and the challenge of personally creative thinking. The students I supervise occasionally say they leave tutorials feeling inspired. It is, I believe, their own inspiration which, through our encounters, they sometimes come to feel again.

References

Becker, S. (1986) *Writing for Social Scientists: How to Start and Finish your Thesis, Book or Article.* University of Chicago Press.

Bogdan, R. C. and Biklen, S. K. (1982) *Qualitative Research for Education: An Introduction to Theory and Method.* Boston, MA: Allyn and Bacon.

Burgess, R. (ed) (1979) *Teaching Research Methodology to Postgraduates: a Survey of Courses in the UK.* Department of Social Science, University of Warwick.

Burgess, R. (ed) (1982) *Field Research: a Sourcebook and Field Manual.* London: Allen and Unwin.

Clayton, K. (1988) 'Recent developments in the funding of university research', *Higher Education Quarterly*, 42, 21.

Cox, R. (1988) *The Characteristics of the Training Process and those Underlying Training.* London: Centre for Higher Education Studies.

Cox, R. et al. (1988) *Research Training in the Social Sciences.* London: Centre of Higher Education Studies.

Glaser, B. G. (1978) *Theoretical Sensitivity.* Chicago Sociology Press.

Gough, H. and Woodworth, D. (1960) 'Stylistic variations among professional research scientists', *Journal of Philosophy*, 49, 152- 155.

Laurillard, D. (1987) 'Computers in the emancipation of students: giving control to the learner', *Institutional Science*, 16, 8- 18.

Lincoln, Y.S and Guba, E.G. (1985) *Naturalistic Enquiry,* California, Sage Publications

Maslow, A. (1985) *The Psychology of Science: a Renaissance.* New York: Harper and Row.

Morris, P. E. (1985) 'The PhD', *Teaching*, 2, 63-68.

Murray, R. (1988) *Training Needs in the Social Sciences and the Effectiveness of Current Provision in Meeting those Needs.* London: ESRC.

Perry, W. (1970) *Forms of Intellectual and Ethical Development in College Years.* New York: Holt, Reinhart and Winston.

Phillips, E. and Pugh, D. (1987) *How to Get a PhD.* Oxford University Press.

Rowan Wilson, J. (1968) 'Research categories', *British Journal of Hospital Medicine,* 1, 134-135.

Rudd, E. (1985) *A New Look at Postgraduate Failure.* London Society for Research in Higher Education.

Schon, D. (1987) *Educating the Reflective Practitioner.* London: Jossey Bass.

Wakeford, J. (1981) 'From methods to practice: a critical note on the teaching of research practice to undergraduates', *Sociology,* 15, 4, 505-512.

Wilson, A. (1987) *Research Progress and Submission Rates: the Social Science PhD.* London: ESRC.

Winfield, G. (1987) *The Social Science PhD: the ESRC Enquiry on Submission Rates.* London: ESRC.

Young, K., McRae, S. and Fogarty, M. (1987) *The Management of Doctoral Studies in the Social Sciences.* London: Policy Studies Institute.